THE
NOVICE RIDER'S

798.23

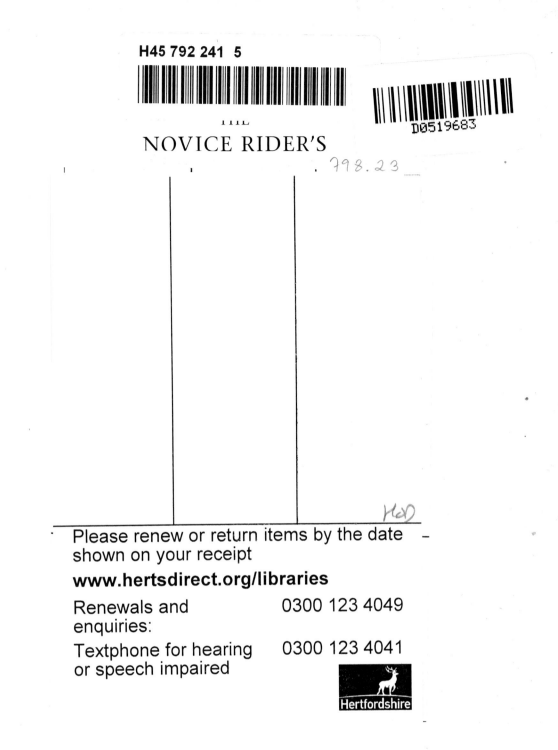

HdD

Please renew or return items by the date
shown on your receipt

www.hertsdirect.org/libraries

Renewals and   0300 123 4049
enquiries:

Textphone for hearing   0300 123 4041
or speech impaired

Hertfordshire

THE NOVICE RIDER'S COMPANION

Principles and Techniques Explained

Martin Diggle

Kenilworth Press

First published in the UK in 2009
by Kenilworth Press, an imprint of Quiller Publishing Ltd

British Library Cataloguing-in-Publication Data
A catalogue record for this book
is available from the British Library

ISBN 978 1 905693 16 0

Illustrations by Maggie Raynor
Designed and typeset by Paul Saunders

Printed in China

Kenilworth Press
An imprint of Quiller Publishing Ltd
Wykey House, Wykey, Shrewsbury, SY4 1JA
Tel: 01939 261616 Fax: 01939 261606
E-mail: info@quillerbooks.com
Website: www.kenilworthpress.co.uk

*To Jayne, whose enthusiasm
to learn more prompted me to write this book*

Contents

Foreword   xi

Introduction   I

Glossary   4

PART 1 **Preliminaries**   II

*This section contains information to cover the period from when
you first think about taking up riding to those first moments in
the saddle.*

Choosing a Riding School   II

Health and Fitness   I4

Basic Equipment   I9

Mounting (and Dismounting)   2I

Assistants and Leaders   24

First Sensations in the Saddle   24

PART 2 **Position and Communication**   29

*This section explains the need to sit correctly, the mechanics of
using the aids, and some principles behind how to apply them
effectively.*

Very Basic Mechanics of the Horse   29

Posture, not Posing   33

A Word About the Seat   41

Using Your Legs   44

Rein Contact   46

A General Note About the Aids and Communication   56

Why They're Called Aids   57

Bossing or Communicating?   58

A Stitch in Time …   59

Timing Aids   62

Showing, not Steering   64

PART 3   **Gaits and Transitions**   70

This section deals with aspects of learning to ride at walk, trot and canter and how to change from one gait to another.

A Word on Walk   70

Rising Trot   73

Sitting Trot   77

Starting to Canter   79

Transitions   84

The Horse's Balance and What 'On the Forehand' Means   92

Half-halts   96

PART 4   **Basic Figures**   99

This section explains the value of riding certain figures and gives some tips on helping to ride them accurately.

Geography and Geometry   99

School Figures   103

Circling   110

Two Lateral Exercises   117

PART 5 **Snippets** 124

This section contains some information and ideas that may be of interest and generally useful as you progress with your riding.

Why the Funny Handshake?	124
Musical Horses	125
Don't Take a 'Tow'	126
Fiddling with Your Straps	127
Uses of a Whip	129
Lunge Lessons	134
Helping to Tack Up	135

PART 6 **Out and About** 137

This section deals with riding beyond the confines of the school.

Riding Out	137
Cantering in the Open	143
Up Hill and Down Dale	153
So, That's the Beginning	157
Useful Addresses	159
Index	160

Foreword

Martin Diggle learned to ride as a young adult and was, for many years, involved with a Riding Club that placed particular emphasis on encouraging membership from adult beginners.

Whilst progressing to competing successfully in dressage, showjumping and cross-country events, he has retained an interest in helping newcomers to riding and has written this book to supplement the knowledge and understanding of novice riders who are in early stages of instruction by professional teachers.

Reading this book in the comfort of their own home will, I am sure, help such riders understand the importance of good posture and correct aids, and thus assist them as they learn to communicate effectively with trained horses.

GEOFF DORSETT BHSI

Former Chief Instructor to the Metropolitan Mounted Police

Introduction

Riding is becoming ever more popular as a sport and recreation, and sensible people are going to licensed riding schools to take lessons from qualified instructors. However, for economic reasons, the normal practice in most schools is to give group lessons, so even the most highly conscientious and competent instructors may have to divide their time between perhaps half a dozen pupils.

This means that it can sometimes be difficult to explain important points in sufficient detail for pupils to really 'get it'. Even when time is allotted for questions at the end of a lesson, these may not form instantly in the mind of a novice who is a bit achy, quite tired and longing for a sit down and a cold drink. In such circumstances, even if one rider asks a question that *should* be of interest to everyone else, it is not always the case that other riders will pay attention to the answer – they might even think it doesn't apply to them. So, questions may not get asked, the answers may not get listened to and in some cases, it must be said, the answer may not be entirely satisfactory.

This combination of circumstances is a major reason why many riders don't progress as rapidly as they might wish – and it is also a reason why bad habits may become ingrained.

Some very eminent trainers have made the point that 'you can't learn riding from a book', and this is very true. Riding is essentially a practical pursuit that involves sitting on a horse and communicating with him, rather than sitting in an armchair, reading. However, it is also true of virtually everything that, in order to do it competently, you first need a reasonable grasp of the key principles. Of course, understanding the theory doesn't *guarantee* that you will put it into practice, but it gives you a chance of doing so. If, on the other hand, you simply try to do something in what is effectively an intellectual vacuum, you have little chance of success, because you don't know what's really important, or why.

So, this book is not a substitute for time in the saddle and it is not intended to replace the need for competent instruction. What it sets out to do is to explain the *importance* of some principles and practices that may get mentioned only in passing during riding lessons, to answer questions that may occur to you at a time when your instructor is not available to answer them, and to deal with some common misconceptions and misunderstandings that might interfere with your progress. It is essentially a beginners' companion that will help you to think about your riding – why you should or shouldn't do certain things – and hopefully it will stimulate you to ask your instructor those questions that were previously just lurking somewhere in the back of your mind.

Because the book is a companion to learning, rather than an 'A to Z' textbook, I have arranged the subject matter into 'Parts' covering broad themes – issues leading up to your first lesson, technical stuff about the aids, riding in the great outdoors, etc. Within each Part, I have tried to arrange the subject matter into the sort of order that readers might be confronted by it, or in which questions may spring to mind. Obviously, this is an inexact science, since different instructors introduce things in slightly different order from each other, and different pupils have their own individual thoughts and queries. Also – and very importantly – although the pupil's and the instructor's *main focus* may be on one particular issue at a time, in riding it is rare (and not usually appropriate) to deal with one issue to the *complete exclusion* of everything else. In recognition of this fact I have, where necessary, made cross-references from one topic to another, and I have given examples of how what a rider does in one particular context may have a material effect on something else. On the basis that readers may be unfamiliar with some of the terminology used in riding (and therefore by their instructors), brief explanations of the most common terms are given in the Glossary.

Before you launch into the main part of this book, there is one other point I would like to make. Most of us, if we are keen to have a go at something, tend to be impatient about matters of detail. That (and the manufacturers' idiosyncratic translations of instructions from their native tongue) is why so many people's flat-pack furniture ends up wonky, and why they can't programme their video-recorders. But if you have that 'impatience' gene and carry it into your riding, there is the chance that, when confronted early on by sections on themes such as 'posture' and 'rein contact', you may be tempted to gloss over them: 'That looks a bit detailed – I'll come back to it later, or figure it out as I go along. How hard can it be to sit on a horse and hold the reins?' Well, just sitting on a horse and holding the reins might not be that difficult, but neither is just sitting in the cockpit of a plane and holding the joystick. But the latter doesn't make you a pilot, and the former doesn't make you a rider. That's why I've written this book – to help you to learn how to do it effectively. So, please, don't be tempted to skip over any bits that look a bit 'heavy' – you might find them really useful.

Glossary

Like most activities, riding has its own jargon. Although good teachers will try to keep this to a minimum, and will doubtless explain terms when asked/when they remember to do so, they will inevitably use *some*, because it is becomes so ingrained in all regular riders. Below, the common terms are explained briefly: I've listed them at the start of the book to provide readers with initial information and to avoid having to interrupt the flow of ideas within the main text. However, some of these terms describe important concepts that are also explored in greater detail in sections of their own.

Within the individual descriptions, when a term is used that also has a glossary entry of its own, this is shown in bold italic.

Active This term is used widely to describe a horse who is moving in a purposeful way, propelling himself in the main by his hindquarters (which are intended for that purpose), stepping forward freely but without hurrying and requiring relatively little encouragement from the rider to maintain his momentum. It implies a basic willingness on the horse's part, and that he is in a reasonable state of balance. Achieving active movement in the *gaits* is a highly desirable goal: in the first place, if the horse is moving with good activity, it is unlikely that the rider is doing anything desperately wrong; second, active movement provides the foundation upon which more advanced riding can take place.

Aids The signals a rider gives to the horse. These are correctly called 'aids' when they are given in a way that helps the horse to recognise and comply with the rider's intentions.

Arena An arena can be a large outdoor or indoor area used for various equestrian sports, such as showjumping and showing classes, but it is also the term generally used for an area of specific size in which dressage competitions take place. There are two sizes of dressage arena: 40 x 20 m and 60 x 20 m, both of which have specific marker letters at set points around their perimeters – it is these markers that form the basis for the movements required in dressage tests. Most riding areas used by riding schools nowadays are, essentially, dressage arenas (see Geography and Geometry in main text) and at these venues the words 'school' and 'arena' are used interchangeably. Some schools and instructors use the French term for riding school, *manège* – this is often rendered incorrectly as *ménage* (which actually means household). See also Note on Measurements at the end of this Glossary.

Bend Lateral flexion (sideways curve) of the horse's body. Because much of his spine is relatively inflexible (much less so than, say, a cat's), the overall 'bend' that a horse achieves to conform to a small circle is actually made up by a number of physical adjustments.

Change the rein This means 'change direction'. Since all good instructors will spend a lot of time and effort convincing pupils that there should be minimal use of the reins in 'steering', this usage could be considered slightly ironic; however, it is a simple and traditional instruction.

Contact see ***rein contact***.

Diagonal This term has two different meanings.

1 A line across the school that is not a 90 degree turn; usually defined by reference to the relevant marker letters (see ***arena***). So, an instructor might say: '***Change the rein*** across the diagonal from F to H' (these being the markers that identify the line required).

2 In the ***gait*** of trot, the horse's legs move in diagonal pairs – the left forefoot and right hind foot together; the right forefoot and left hind foot together. These are commonly referred to as 'the diagonals'.

Form a ride This means that everyone on the lesson should proceed round the ***outside track*** of the school in single file, at walk, usually with a horse's length between horses. The message 'with [rider's/horse's name] as *leading file*' (see that entry) is often added to this instruction.

Gait A distinctive mode of progression of the horse, characterised by a certain sequence of footfalls. Most horses have four gaits – walk, trot, canter and gallop. Some breeds have different gaits than these, which may be more or less natural, or developed by special training, but these are not normally seen in horses used in the riding school. Many people call the gaits '*paces*', but this is a rather imprecise term, which can be confused with references to speed or individual steps. In some circumstances, it may also be confused with one of the unusual gaits which, itself, is called 'pacing'.

Go large Not a command to develop Michelin man proportions, but to proceed around the *outside track*.

Impulsion Impulsion means that a horse is moving forward in good balance from the powerful, controlled thrusting of his hindquarters 'let through' rather than 'blocked' by the rest of his body . In simple terms, it might be described as '*Activity +*'.

Inside (leg, hand, rein, etc.) The term 'inside' refers to the concave side of any lateral *bend* in the horse. At a basic level, in the vast majority of cases, this inside bend will be towards the centre of the school, so in these cases the inside leg, etc., will be the one nearer the centre of the school. At a more advanced level, however, horses are sometimes asked to perform movements in which the inside bend of their body is towards the *outside* of the school. Because of this, it is worth becoming familiar with the correct use: inside always means 'of the horse'; it does not *inevitably* mean 'of the school'.

Inside track The track about a horse's width to the inside of, and parallel to, the *outside track*. Riding around the inside track is a very good exercise in controlling the horse's straightness, because the outside track has a kind of 'magnetic attraction' for horses – they are usually ridden round the outside track and they instinctively gravitate towards it. If you can ride reasonably straight and actively around the inside track, this is evidence that you have the horse's attention and that you are applying the *aids* effectively.

Leading file The horse and rider at the front of a ride (see *form a ride*). While it was traditional for instructors to refer to the person at the front as 'leading file' ('Leading file, trot on, etc.'), many nowadays adopt a less formal approach and use the rider's (or horse's) name.

On the forehand This describes a horse who is more or less 'pulling' himself along with his forelegs and shoulders, rather than 'pushing' himself along with his hind legs and hindquarters. There are various reasons why a horse might do this. One is a matter of conformation: there are some horses with big, heavy shoulders and weak back ends; some have an abnormally high back end ('croup-high') which tends to tip them forwards, and some have hind legs of a shape that makes it difficult for them to 'engage' underneath the horse. However, by far the most frequent cause of a horse being on his forehand is that the rider allows or induces this way of moving. Factors relating to this are discussed in the main text under The Horse's Balance and What 'On the Forehand' Means.

On the left rein Going anticlockwise.

On the right rein Going clockwise.

Open order For pupils at an early stage, riding in open order will usually mean that, rather than proceeding as a *ride* (quite close together), horses and riders will be spread more or less evenly round the *outside track*, all on the same rein (going in the same direction) and going at the same *gait*. At a more advanced stage, it may signify riders changing direction and gait according to their wishes. Obviously, this cannot be done safely until everyone involved is in full control of their individual horse, and fully aware of what is going on around them. If you go to a local show, and watch riders in the warm-up arena, you will see riding in open order, often with unedifying results.

Outside (leg, hand, rein, etc.) The term 'outside' refers to the convex side of any lateral *bend* in the horse and is thus the opposite of *inside*. At a basic level, in the vast majority of cases, this outside bend will be towards the perimeter of the school, so the outside leg, etc. will be the one further from the centre of the school. However, this is not *always* the case – see note on **inside**.

Outside track Not a track outside the school, but the widest practical route around its internal perimeter – i.e. a track half a metre or so in from the wall or fence.

Paces see **gait**.

Rear file The horse and rider at the back of a **ride**.

Rein contact The connection between the rider's hands and the horse's mouth, via the reins and bit. Commonly abbreviated to '**contact**'.

Tack Not an instruction to zigzag up the school like a yacht in a gale, but a traditional term for the saddle, bridle and associated gear. Fitting this prior to riding is called 'tacking up'. Items of tack that might require further adjustment before mounting (and sometimes during a lesson) are the girth and stirrup leathers. The girth is the strap that holds the saddle in place and many horses are adept at 'blowing themselves out' when this is first fastened, which means that, by the time they are mounted (and perhaps after they've done a bit of work), the girth will be looser than desirable. For this reason, it is important to check the girth before mounting and again after ten minutes or so. The instructor should make pupils aware of this and, in the early stages, carry out the checks on their behalf. The length of the stirrup leathers will influence the ease (or otherwise) of mounting and the position of the rider's legs and, again, is something the instructor should advise upon.

The ride/the whole ride These terms have been used traditionally to mean 'everyone on the lesson, together': 'The whole ride trot on'; 'Ride, halt', etc.

Transition A change from one **gait** to another, or to and from halt. For the scope of this book, this will be a simple transition from one gait to the next one 'up' or 'down'. However, with experience, you will be able to 'miss a gear' – e.g. go directly from walk into canter, trot into halt, etc.

Experienced riders on well-trained horses can also ride transitions 'within the gait', i.e. lengthen or shorten the horse's strides a prescribed amount *within* the existing gait.

Wrong bend A comment that may be made by an instructor when a pupil is riding on a circle or through a corner incorrectly. In all normal, basic circumstances, when on a circle or going through a corner (usually ridden as a quarter of a circle), the horse should be bent (see ***bend***) along the line of the figure – i.e. his inside should be to the inside of the figure. Wrong bend occurs when the rider's aids allow or cause the horse to be bent in the opposite direction.

    NB There are certain advanced movements, intended to improve suppleness, in which the horse is deliberately ridden with his ***inside*** bend to the *outside of the figure*. Done intentionally, this is known as counter-bend.

Wrong leg/lead The ***gait*** of canter has an asymmetrical sequence of footfalls, whereby one or other of the horse's forelegs moves individually as the 'leading leg'. When going through a corner/on a circle, to assist balance this leading leg should be to the ***inside*** (e.g. right foreleg leading when circling to the right). However, perhaps because he is confused by the rider's ***aids*** or by accidental shifts of weight, a horse may start cantering on the lead that is wrong for the intended movement. On noticing this, an instructor will say 'Wrong leg' or 'Wrong lead' and tell the pupil to return to trot before asking again for the correct canter lead.

Note on Measurements
Most general measurements in this book are given in imperial units, but since – as mentioned under ***arena*** – schooling areas are usually contructed to metric dimensions, it is traditional to give the measurements of school figures in metric units (e.g. 20 m circles, 5 m loops).

PART 1

Preliminaries

This section contains information to cover the period from when you first think about taking up riding to those first moments in the saddle.

Choosing a Riding School

If you have not already done so before reading this book, your first act will be to choose a riding school. There are various factors that will influence your choice and, since these will differ in some respects for each individual, the following are just some pointers to throw into the mix. In the first place, as with restaurants, pubs, holiday resorts, etc., nearest is not necessarily best. Second, as with the facilities just mentioned, personal recommendation (or otherwise) can be a good guide.

The most fundamental point about any UK establishment purporting to be a riding school is that it must be licensed by the local authority. Since this licence is renewable annually, subject to an inspection, the possession of a current licence gives some sort of indication in respect of matters such as proprietorial/managerial experience, animal welfare, public liability insurance, public health and fire regulations, etc. A list of licensed schools in their area should be available from the relevant local authority and legitimate schools usually display their licence somewhere prominent.

While this licensing is the only legal requirement for establishing their legitimate status, many UK schools are also voluntarily linked to one or both of two other organisations – the British Horse Society (BHS) and the Association of British Riding Schools (ABRS). In short, the BHS is the body that promotes riding as a sport and recreation in Britain, while the ABRS is basically a trade association of riding school proprietors. Both these organisations are interested in promoting good standards and practice and both carry out annual inspections of riding schools affiliated to them. While these inspections have some criteria similar to those of the licensing authority, they are distinct from the latter and place additional emphasis on teaching standards. Schools which have passed inspections by these bodies will display relevant plaques – a blue plaque identifying the current year of inspection in the case of the BHS and a white triangle in the case of the ABRS.

These matters aside, personal assessment is also important. You may think that, as a beginner, you are not in a position to sit in judgement about the running of a riding school and, to some extent, that is so. However, as with buying a house or joining a club, a mixture of gut instinct and common sense can help inform your decision. Telephone the school, say that you are thinking of starting lessons, inquire about times, availability, class sizes and prices, and ask if you can go along and watch a novice lesson. You may learn quite a lot from the way in which your inquiry is received and dealt with – if it seems unwelcoming you may be better off looking elsewhere. (Incidentally, phoning first is a better option than dropping in unannounced. These days, with thefts of tack and horses being so prevalent, riding establishments have to remain vigilant, so calling beforehand and introducing yourself when you go to the yard will be seen as acts of courtesy.)

When you arrive, all being well, someone will show you around and you will get a chance to see a lesson in progress. At this time, you will be in a position to soak up the atmosphere. As mentioned, while you may not feel competent to judge all aspects of what is going on, the following are points you can definitely consider:

- The overall atmosphere should feel friendly and reasonably efficient. There should be a sense that staff are co-operating with each other, and that lessons are running more or less on time.

- Although riding schools may get a little untidy at busy times, the place shouldn't look shambolic, dangerous or post-apocalyptic.

- Horses looking over stable doors with pricked ears and amiable demeanours are a good sign – nervous or aggressive-looking horses are not.

- Bedding in stables should look reasonably deep, dry and clean. Inevitably, some may contain the odd pile of recently-passed dung, but there should be no large accumulations unattended to.

- On watching a lesson, you should get an overall impression of good communication between instructor and pupils – a little friendly banter is fine, but you don't want to see an instructor shouting at confused or worried pupils. While a horse may occasionally 'take the mickey' in some mild manner (cutting a corner, or being a little slow to respond to the rider), you don't want to see evidence of anything that could be characterised as bad behaviour (no horses bucking, rearing or danger-ously out of control). The bottom line is, you want to be thinking: 'That looks fun – I fancy having a go', not: 'Sod that for a game of soldiers, I'll stick to wrestling alligators.'

- The structure of the school itself is worth considering. The surface should be pretty level, with no deeply worn entrenchments around the perimeter. A composite 'all-weather' surface (usually a mixture of rubber and coarse sand) is much preferable to woodchip or plain sand. Wood surfaces can get very deep and loose and, if exposed to frost, they can form 'mats' that may move loosely and dangerously beneath the horses' hooves. Deep, dry sand makes hard work for the horses (and thus, the riders), and is also dusty – and sand schools almost always freeze at some stage during the winter, which can lead to lessons being cancelled. Generally, a covered (or fully indoor) school is a boon to riders, because both surface and riders are protected from the rigours of the elements. However, some enclosed schools can get very dusty (and hot in summer) and these may not be suitable for someone with a condition such as asthma (see section on Health and Fitness).

If, having checked these points, you think that a particular school might suit you, one other thing to consider is cost. It is, at least, a consideration for most people and you should bear in mind that, if you are to make progress, you will need to have lessons on a regular basis (as a general guide, many people have them weekly). Obviously, everyone's financial circumstances vary, but here are a couple of observations that may be helpful:

- Really good lessons that you can just afford are much better value than poor, but affordable lessons. As with everything, value is not simply a matter of price.

- That said, there is not necessarily an equation that says expensive = good; inexpensive = poor. There are some relatively inexpensive schools that offer very good value, and there are others that charge the earth and don't really deliver.

In other words:

Don't choose a school *just because it's a cheap option.*

Don't *assume* that a school will be good *just because it's expensive.*

So, while cost may well be a significant factor in making your choice, don't let it be the overriding one. As I said at the start of this section, there are many variables to consider when choosing a riding school but, ultimately, your own instincts may be the best guide of all – after all, it's your time and your money, and you will be most receptive to learning in an environment where you are happy.

Health and Fitness

Don't worry – I'm not going to launch into a series of horror stories about people being devoured by wild stallions, or suggest that you shouldn't go anywhere near a horse without wearing plate armour – I'm just going to deal with a few practical, commonsense points that may be of value to newcomers to riding.

The first point is that, in common with most physical activities, riding is likely to prove easier for people who are reasonably fit, in good health and able-bodied – and throughout the rest of this book, the assumption is made that this is true of the reader. However, if it is not so in your case, this does not necessarily mean that you cannot enjoy riding, given an appropriate approach. In fact, many people with conditions that would compromise learning to ride through standard channels gain enormous satisfaction from the sport through the work of the Riding for the Disabled Association (RDA). This charitable organisation has a UK-wide network of centres with specially trained instructors and dedicated helpers and it assists people with a wide spectrum of disabilities to ride to the highest level practicable – often with truly amazing results. Further information can be obtained from the RDA at Lavinia Norfolk House, Avenue R, Stoneleigh Park, Stoneleigh, Kenilworth, Warwickshire, CV8 2LY (tel: 0845 658 1082, website www.rda.org.uk).

If you are well most of the time but suffer from a medical condition that might intermittently incapacitate you, then you should tell your GP that you would like to start riding and take note of any advice given. Assuming that you get the go-ahead, inform the manager of the riding school *and* your instructor of your condition and, if appropriate, keep a note about your condition and a dose of any medication you may require about your person whilst riding (the latter not, of course, in a glass container!)

It is worth noting that riding requires more physical effort than many people imagine and you should be aware of this if you have any condition that compromises circulation or breathing. People with breathing difficulties should be aware that, in addition to the physical demands of riding, riding schools can be dusty environments – as well as the dust from arena surfaces, there will be horse hair, scurf, and dust from hay and bedding to contend with. Again, it may be worth mentioning these factors in any discussion with your GP.

If you suffer from any 'wear and tear' conditions – especially of the leg joints and back – these should also be given due consideration. A weak ankle may well be helped by a support bandage (provided you can get your boot on over it) and problems with a dodgy hip may well be minimised by riding a fairly narrow horse. Back problems, it must be said, are never good news for riding, since it is an enormous help if your lower back is in good nick to act as a 'shock absorber' and – as you progress – you will find that you can use your back in various ways to help control the horse. However, there are devices available to help support bad backs (you'll probably know this already, if you have an ongoing problem) and it is a matter of fact that, by virtue of their build and movement, some horses are inherently more comfortable to ride than others.

Again, if you have any conditions of this sort, *tell the instructor.* No instructor worth their salt will think you are 'making excuses' or 'wimping out' if you inform them of a genuine physical problem. Instead, they will be glad of the information because a good instructor would be mortified to think he or she had been 'getting on the case' of a pupil in real difficulty. Rather than unwittingly risk discomfort or damage to a pupil, they would rather try to find a way of accommodating the condition – but they have to know about it first.

These days, there are many pressures in the commercial world and one consequence of this is that people often feel obliged to work when they are distinctly 'under the weather'. So far as riding is concerned (which readers of this book will be doing for recreation and *pleasure*), I would advise against extending workplace obligations to the riding school. If you've got a bit of a head cold and you think that some fresh air and exercise might do you good, that's one thing. But, if you feel distinctly rough, give it a miss. If, for example, you are muzzy-headed, your reactions will be slower than usual and your communication with the horse will be ineffective and, if you are feeling a bit weak, you will tend to 'hang on' and become a passenger and a burden to the horse, rather than a proactive partner. *If you ever misjudge your condition and find yourself feeling dizzy or faint on a horse, tell your instructor at once, and get off as soon as you can do so safely.*

Falls

I was very much in two minds about whether to mention this subject, since I was concerned that it might send a negative message. However, this book is a companion for novices and I think that, realistically, the possibility of falling off is something that goes (albeit fleetingly) through the minds of a significant proportion of people about to take up riding. For most people, I think this has much more to do with concerns about 'cocking it up' or appearing foolish than actual fear – it has much in common with the newcomer to skiing or ice skating who wonders how long it will be before they go flat on their backside, or the novice golfer at the Pro-Am who is hoping he won't miss the ball on the first tee in front of a crowd of thousands. Despite all the advice about positive thinking from life coaches and sport psychologists, such thought processes have yet to be eradicated from the human psyche. So, let's give the possibility of coming off a little consideration at this point – and then dismiss it from our minds.

First, it is a fact that riding contains an element of risk and to claim that no one ever gets hurt doing it would be simply untrue. Also, it has to be said that, for anyone who rides regularly, the probability exists that they will come off for some reason, at some time. Finally, since each incident has its own circumstances, generalisations about the likely outcome can be no more than that. However, here are some observations that may help to put any concerns into some context.

- Although no one ever intends to fall off a horse, there are various other popular sports in which hurling yourself to the ground (or being hurled) are part and parcel of participation. Obvious examples include martial arts, rugby, football, cricket (even tennis, if you're Nadalesque) – and (although falling whilst doing them is involuntary) the aforementioned skiing and ice skating must count as virtual certainties for most people. Anyone who engages regularly and enthusiastically in such sports should have no qualms at all about riding, so far as frequency of meeting the ground is concerned.

- Accredited riding schools and qualified instructors in the UK are, nowadays, very safety-conscious and will take great care that horses, equipment and the instruction given are as safe as practicable. (Equipment includes what the pupils are wearing – see Basic Equipment.) Thus the chances of a beginner coming off as a result of equipment failure or a horse really 'playing up' should be extremely remote.

- Sitting on a horse who is moving steadily and rhythmically is not really a precarious process (since he has a leg at each corner and no interest in falling over himself, it is much less precarious than riding a two-wheeled vehicle). If you pay attention to matters of posture (see Posture, not Posing) and the advice of your instructor, there is no real reason why you *should* come off a sedately moving horse.

- If you *do* have the misfortune to come off early in your riding career, you will be falling from a modest height, at moderate speed onto a reasonably forgiving surface. In these circumstances, it will be a considerable misfortune if you suffer any significant injury.

- If you *are* unfortunate enough to be hurt, qualified instructors nowadays have first aid training, and the instructor and school management will ensure that any medical support necessary is summoned promptly.

- In the vast majority of cases, no significant damage is done. Once you and the instructor, jointly, have ascertained that this is so, it is simply a question of dusting yourself down, getting back on and continuing. However, there are a few supplementary points to this:

1 No sensible instructor is going to persuade a pupil to remount if the pupil doesn't feel up to it – but you shouldn't pretend to be all right if you know you're not. Forget anything you may have heard about fallen riders having to get straight back on or they'll 'lose their nerve'. Apart from the fact that this is complete nonsense, it is far better for a rider who wishes to put a mishap behind them to return to the saddle fully functional, than to be struggling with some incapacity.

2 In some cases, if a rider is temporarily incapacitated but not really injured (winded, for example) it may be appropriate for them to rest for a while until they've regained their breath and composure, and then finish up with a few quiet minutes back in the saddle. This is great if it proves all right to do so, but is a 'wait and see' matter that shouldn't be prejudged either way.

3 For reasons given earlier, in most cases when novice riders fall off this is because they've done something that compromised their own balance. In plainer terms, they've done something wrong. In such a case, in the pupil's interests, the instructor has a duty to tell the pupil what has happened and why. Obviously, the instructor should be diplomatic about this, but if it happens to you, it is far more sensible to listen and try to correct the error than to adopt a self-pitying 'Blimey, I've just gone arse-first and now he/she's having a go at me' approach.

Hopefully, these points will dispel any lurking concerns and when we come to the section First Sensations in the Saddle your sensations will all be positive and you won't feel inclined to make any of the errors that can be associated with feelings of insecurity. So, enough about falls. From now on, let's concentrate on getting into the saddle and enjoying being there.

Basic Equipment

When you first approach your chosen school, you will doubtless be given a rundown of what will and won't serve as riding attire until you buy the proper gear, but here are a few brief thoughts.

- Any riding school remotely worth its licence will insist that, when riding, you wear a hard hat approved to current safety standards. Many schools keep, and sell, these hats – and they are also available from tack shops. Size, fit and adjustment of this headgear is important and reputable outlets will have staff trained to give informed advice on these matters.

- Body protectors were originally developed to protect jockeys, and their key function remains to protect a rider from a heavy fall, from being rolled on by the horse, or from the hooves of other horses. Hopefully, these threats are pretty remote to a beginner at a riding school and, unlike hard hats, body protectors are not standard requisites in the school environment. Protective functions aside, they are somewhat restrictive of movement and hot to wear. However, if you have a physical condition that requires particular protection, or are otherwise anxious about the possibilities of a fall, by all means wear one. As with hats, informed assistance can help with matters of style and fit.

- Although you *can* ride in ordinary trousers, jeans and jogging bottoms, these are all uncomfortable to a greater or lesser extent. Tight jeans will make your eyes water and all these items (with the possible exception of proper stretch-fit tracksuit bottoms) will ruck up and rub your legs. All will suffer a great deal of wear and tear. As soon as you've decided that riding is for you, buy a proper pair of jodhpurs or breeches – you don't need top-of-the-range ones and there are some good second-hand outlets around.

- Long boots are the best footwear and, although they're a bit rudimentary and won't last that long, you can buy basic rubber riding boots quite cheaply. These will do until you fancy moving upmarket to posher versions or leather boots, and they'll enable you to walk through puddles and piles of droppings with relative impunity. Don't buy any that are obviously a tight fit – cramp on horseback is not fun. Some people prefer short boots – these were traditionally called jodhpur boots or dealer boots but are now marketed under many different trade names. They will probably be more comfortable on your feet than long rubber boots, but they give less support and less of a 'solid' feeling to your lower legs. Purpose-built footwear aside, there is nothing really suitable in the short term except what used to be called 'stout walking shoes' – and not many people own these nowadays. *Don't* wear wellies – they will be uncomfortable and are potentially dangerous, since their extra width makes them prone to getting stuck in the stirrups. They can also get caught under the saddle flaps, and rub the horse's sides. Shoes with bigger than average heels are potentially dangerous since, if a foot slips through a stirrup, the heel might trap your foot. Trainers are too insubstantial and there is a risk that they might slide dangerously right through the stirrups. They are, in fact, a no-no around stable yards – ask anyone who's ever had a foot trodden on by a horse whilst wearing them.

- Gloves are useful, especially in hot, humid weather, when horses can get sweaty or, alternatively, in the wet. Actual safety (potential for breakage) aside, the type and condition of reins used in some schools leaves something to be desired and gloves can assist a comfortable hold of the reins. You don't need anything expensive – most tack shops sell basic rubber-palmed gloves for under a fiver.

- Many beginners think that carrying a whip is pretentious; that it will clutter up their hand and that they will be more likely to poke themselves in the eye with it than do anything useful in terms of horse-encouragement. In the very early stages, there is probably something in the cluttering theory but, although it shouldn't be necessary to use a whip extensively (and very rarely for punishment), the whip has a legitimate role in backing up aids from the rider's legs. It is therefore worthwhile obtaining one at a fairly early stage and getting used to handling it. (For information on types and how to use them, see Uses of a Whip.)

Mounting (and Dismounting)

You cannot, of course, ride a horse without first getting on board, and at some stage you will need to get off again. There are easy and difficult, safe and precarious ways of doing both, and an instructor may spend some time on these processes. In addition to increasing proficiency, practising mounting and dismounting will help a beginner make the physical and mental adjustments between ground and horse.

Most riding schools will provide a mounting block to aid the getting on process. A mounting block is just a sturdy step, either fixed or movable, a foot or so high. Standing on it raises the rider relative to the horse's back and makes the process of mounting easier. Although it is useful to be able to mount from the ground (something worth practising in due course), most experienced riders will still use a mounting block if one is available, because doing so places less strain on the saddlery and also on the horse's physique. Do not, therefore, think that being pre-sented with a mounting block is a badge of incompetence – it isn't, and it's always preferable to use one.

Prior to starting the process of mounting, it is very sound practice to check the girth (the strap that holds the saddle in place). Certainly, in the early stages, your instructor should point this out and assist you. It will also be helpful to check that the stirrup leathers are adjusted to a length more or less suitable for your physique. If they are significantly too long for you, this will hinder the process of swinging into the saddle; if they are significantly too short they will, again, hinder the mounting process (if you *don't* have access to a mounting block, they will make it excep-tionally difficult) and, once on board, they will make you feel like a jockey which, at the first time of mounting, may feel precarious. 'But', you ask, 'if I've not yet sat on the horse, how will I know what length the stirrup leathers should be?' Well, there's a rule of thumb that works as a rough guide for most people (that your instructor will doubtless be aware of). The length of your straight arm from fist to armpit will be more or less (give or take a hole or so) the length of stirrup leather that will suit your legs. So, if you keep your arm straight and put your fist against the stirrup bar (the metal bar through which the stirrup leather is fastened to the saddle), the stirrup leather will be about right if the bottom of the stirrup just reaches your armpit. (Fine adjustments can be made once you're on board.)

Certainly for the first few times of mounting, there will be someone on hand to ensure that the horse stands still during the process and, in due course, your instructor will explain how you can help keep him still yourself. (Riding school horses shouldn't be unduly fidgety to mount, but horses aren't blocks of stone and you can't guarantee that every horse you ride will stand as though rooted to the spot.)

For historical and traditional reasons, it is usual to mount from and dismount to the horse's near side (left). Even if you have the assistance of a decent mounting block, the mounting process is made easier if, with your left foot in the stirrup, you make a fairly determined effort to spring up from your right foot. A good spring with that foot will aid the process of swinging it clear over the horse's back, which is vastly preferable for the horse than to have you kick him in the side, and vastly preferable from your viewpoint than to find that your right leg is snagged up against the horse's back or the rear of the saddle (the cantle). Springing from the right foot also avoids dragging yourself into the saddle by putting excessive weight on the left foot in the stirrup, a method that places considerable strain on both the tack and the horse, and makes you look like a drunken brontosaurus trying to heave its way out of a primeval swamp.

Assuming that you are safely on board, we'll jump ahead for a moment to the time when you wish to dismount. To do so safely, the horse should be standing still and, again, in the early stages there should be someone available to assist you. Dismounting, like mounting, is done most easily and cleanly if there is some measure of commitment. Basic-ally, you take both reins in your left hand, rest this on the horse's withers (just in front of the saddle), lean (don't curl) your upper body forward, then swing both legs backwards with some vigour. This vigour has to be sufficient to allow you to swing your right leg up and over the back of the saddle (and the horse's back) with an impetus that will return you to the ground feet first. Be warned – if you don't commit to this, you will catch your leg on the saddle and slide off in a heap.

As stated, it is usual to mount from the near side and to return to that side on dismounting. However, it can be useful (in confined spaces or some kind of emergency) to be able to mount from and dismount to the off side, and (once you are proficient with the normal process) sensi-ble instructors will teach you how to do this and will get you to practise it from time to time.

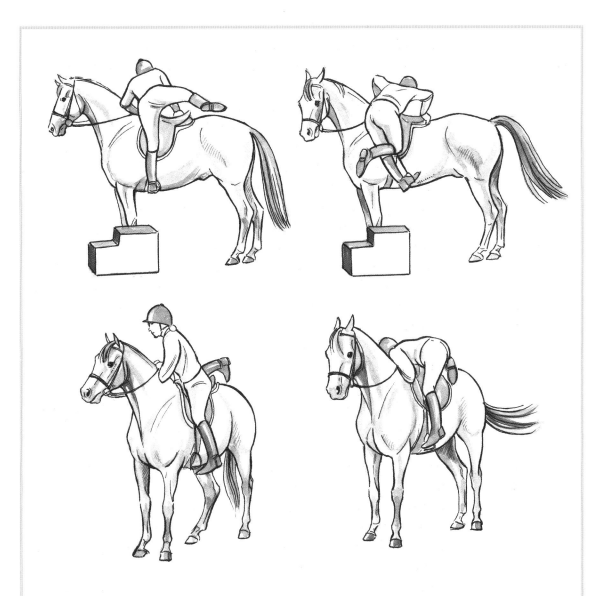

Correct (*left*) and incorrect (*right*) ways of mounting and dismounting. *Top left*: rider springing up from the right leg and swinging it clear over the saddle. *Top right*: rider's weight in left stirrup; rider hanging on to cantle of saddle – awkward and uncomfortable for horse and rider and places strain on tack. *Bottom left*: rider swings right leg up and clear of cantle, to land balanced on both feet. *Bottom right*: lack of commitment when dismounting means that rider will get 'caught up' on the saddle and is likely to land in a heap.

Assistants and Leaders

For beginners' first lessons, some riding schools provide assistants to lead the horses from the ground. Whether or not a particular school does this probably relates to its basic philosophy and the availability or otherwise of helpers. Typically, helpers will be either working pupils (studying for professional qualifications at the yard) or other keen youngsters giving a hand in return for some rides for themselves. If you find yourself, on your first couple of rides, being escorted around the school by someone the same age as your own children, you shouldn't consider this demeaning. At a very early stage, having someone sensible to keep the horse going smoothly will leave you free to concentrate on your position in the saddle, holding the reins correctly and the overall sensations of being in motion. In principle, early assistance of this sort has similarities to riding on the lunge (see Lunge Lessons), in which the instructor keeps the horse moving on a circle while you hone your position.

Another arrangement that can be of assistance to a class of beginners is to have a more experienced rider as 'leading file'. Again, this might well be a working pupil who can also benefit personally from observing the teaching technique of the instructor. Such a person, at the front of the ride, can help to regulate speed and can also be used by the instructor to demonstrate various points. Having someone available who can give a reasonable indication of 'what it should look like' is a considerable help to teacher and pupils alike.

First Sensations in the Saddle

If you have made the decision to have a go at riding, it's a fair assumption that, even if you're completely unfamiliar with horses, you have at least a basic liking for them, and are expecting (or, at least, hoping) to enjoy the experience. In practice, most people actively enjoy the first sensation of sitting on a horse's back, and very few people are seriously worried by it, but a general feeling of *unfamiliarity* is by no means unusual – for the very good reason that, for first-timers, it is an unfamiliar sensation. Horses themselves, being fundamentally prey animals, are programmed by their instincts to be suspicious of anything or circumstance with which they are unfamiliar. Human beings, while not in the same position as horses, are highly sentient and observant, and (unless we've been on the home brew) we all register new situations and sensations automatically. Imagine mistakenly putting on shoes from two different pairs; even though they're the same size and colour, you'd notice before you'd taken more than a step or two – probably earlier.

When you sit on a horse for the first time, there are two obvious differences from 'normal life' to notice. The first is that you are somewhat higher up than normal, and the second is an awareness that (even though he's standing still and quiet), you are astride a living creature, capable of moving of his own volition. In the interest of preparing your brain's responses to these noted differences, let's put them into context.

- When a person is sitting on a horse, their 'extra' height above the ground is not the full height of the horse – it is a slightly less than the distance from their feet in the stirrups to the ground (slightly less because, when standing on the ground, their legs will be straighter than when sitting in the saddle). For most people on most horses, this distance will be less than 3 feet – so, in terms of height, sitting on a horse approximates to standing on your dining room table to change a light bulb.

- The fact that the horse is capable of moving is the fundamental reason why you want to ride him – if you wanted to sit on something that kept still, you'd have chosen a park bench.

So, you're not actually very high up, and you've made a conscious choice to sit on a moving animal. Many first-timers, when asked how they feel at this point, respond with a 'Feels great, let's go' attitude. However, there are some people who respond to the general unfamiliarity of their situation by feeling a little insecure at first. If you are one of the latter, don't feel down about it – no one's gung-ho about everything and the guy on the horse next to you, who's coming on like a cross between John Wayne and Frankie Dettori, may be scared of his mother-in-law.

Nevertheless, if you do feel at all insecure, it is necessary to acknowledge that some of the natural human responses to *feelings* of insecurity can be counter-productive to both *actual* security and effective riding, so it is necessary to take this on board and dissipate these feelings at an early stage. A conscientious, effective instructor can be a great help, both psychologically and physically, in dealing with the following points and instilling confidence. *These points should be studied by even the most confident beginners, because some of them might arise unconsciously, or from simple misconception.*

General tension Insecurity often causes general tension and thus stiffness in the body. Because it will affect a rider's seat, legs and hands, this tension blocks effective communication with the horse and, since horses are sensitive to such things, the horse will also pick it up. (In a sensible riding school horse, this will not produce any major reactions, but he will pick it up, nonetheless.) Significantly, tension in the buttock muscles will cause a rider to bounce around in the saddle and this will significantly *reduce* security. Experienced instructors will have their own words of wisdom (beyond saying 'Relax') and perhaps basic exercises designed to reduce initial tension.

The desire to grip When people feel insecure, they have an instinctive and perfectly logical desire to grip something. For someone on a horse, the most obvious things to grip – since they are already holding them – are the reins. Now, obvious this might be, but helpful (or even logical) it is not. In fact, one of the biggest favours you can do for yourself as a rider is to convince yourself, from the very beginning, that *the reins are not for hanging on by*. This, in fact, also means doing a big favour to any horses you ride, but for the moment let's just think about *your* situation. If you really want to hang on to something that will increase your security in the saddle, then logic dictates that this must be something that draws you closer to it. The only directions in which you can pull the reins are backwards or upwards, neither of which achieves the desired effect and either of which may embroil you in a pulling match with an uncomfortable, upset horse. And, since the horse is six or seven times bigger and stronger than you, this is a pulling match you will lose – and the horse will be pulling you forwards and down…

In terms of drawing you closer to the saddle, the best thing to hold on to is the saddle itself and the instructor may recommend that, if you feel at all insecure, you grasp the front arch of the saddle with one hand. At certain stages, in fact, you might find the instructor telling pupils to do this as part of an exercise in improving posture and 'depth of seat'. (As an alternative security measure, some schools provide neckstraps –

usually spare stirrup leathers fastened loosely round the horses' necks. These have some value, but it may be compromised by a tendency for pupils curling forwards a little to use them to: if they do this, it reduces the security of the seat.)

Apart from the hands, the other parts of their anatomy with which pupils can grip are the legs. As with trying to hang on by the reins this is, in most circumstances, counter-productive. The basic reason for this is that, for the horse, pressure from the rider's legs is a signal to move forwards. A substantial application of pressure (sustained gripping) may be interpreted by the horse as a requirement to move forwards suddenly and quickly – not the best response for a rider who is feeling insecure.

This is not to say that the rider's legs shouldn't be in *contact* with the horse. In most situations they should be (see Use of Legs, later), but *resting against his sides*, not clamped on. In *an emergency* (serious loss of balance or a horse really misbehaving) strong gripping may well be justified, but there are a few points relating to this:

1 Such an occurrence is unlikely in a well-run lesson for novice riders.

2 *Resolving* bad behaviour usually requires the employment of additional riding skills – *just* clamping the legs on (although it might aid the rider's stability in the saddle) is still, fundamentally, a crude signal for the horse to go forwards.

3 Gripping with the legs (when necessary) is far more effective in riders who have already established a good position in the saddle through the use of their seat, than in beginners who have not yet done so. This is because, in experienced riders, the stability of their position (called a 'deep seat') involves really sitting 'into' the saddle with their legs hanging long down the horse's sides, with the facility to 'wrap around' the horse. Most beginners, on the other hand, will instinctively try to create grip on the widest part of the horse, by bringing their lower legs up – but doing this may result in their feet coming out of the stirrups and the security of their position being *decreased*.

To counteract any tendency for pupils to 'grip up' with their legs, a good instructor will explain that constructive use of the forces of gravity, rather than gripping, is the key to security. If you are sitting upright on a horse, gravity will be pulling the whole weight of your upper body vertically down into the saddle, more or less 'sticking' you to the saddle. If you then allow your long, heavy legs to hang down freely on each side of the horse, their weight (and its position below your seat) will add significantly to this effect. In short, you are *letting* yourself be secure.

Some advice on the key points of posture and how to hold the reins, followed by some simple practical experience of starting, stopping and turning in walk, is likely to form the basis of your first lesson. Most instructors are, at this stage, primarily concerned with getting pupils used to the sensation of being on a moving horse. As lessons progress, you will learn more about the details of position, applying the aids, riding simple figures and moving on to trotting and cantering. Information and advice on these topics appears in the later sections of this book.

PART 2

Position and Communication

This section explains the need to sit correctly, the mechanics of using the aids, and some principles behind how to apply them effectively.

Very Basic Mechanics of the Horse

This part of the book will deal with fundamentals of how to influence the horse, both in terms of the rider's own 'mechanisms' (position, hands and legs) and how these can be applied thoughtfully, constructively and effectively. However, before one makes any serious attempt to influence any conveyance, it is useful to have a very basic idea of 'how it goes'. This applies to all sorts of things, from sailing boats to gliders but, to take a more common example, if you are going to learn to drive a car with a manual gearbox, it helps to know a little bit about what gears are *for*, and how they relate to the power produced by the engine. To develop this idea further, if you are learning to ride a bicycle, you need to find out what gears are for pretty quickly, because *you* are the engine! It also helps if you know enough to inflate the tyres, check the tension of the chain and make sure that the brakes aren't binding, because all these things can affect mechanical efficiency – and how hard you have to work.

So far as riding is concerned, it is not the specifics of 'gears' I'm going to discuss here, but the more general matter of mechanical ease and difficulty. Fundamentally, you can ride a horse in a way that makes it either easy or difficult for him to carry your weight and move freely. And, although a rider is not the 'engine' of a horse in the way that a cyclist is of a bike, if you make things hard for the horse, you will certainly end up expending a great deal of effort yourself, for very little reward.

If you look at a horse as though he were a mechanical structure, you will see that the main part of his body is a bit like a suspension bridge – the pillars of the bridge are his forelegs and shoulders at one end, and his hind legs and hindquarters at the other end. Between these, his spine represents the span of the bridge. Now, it is a fact of structural engineering that a convexly (upward) arched bridge is considerably stronger than a concave (sagging) one, and is thus capable of bearing greater weight. Transposing this fact to the horse, it is clear that, if we can encourage him to round his back upwards a little, as opposed to dropping it ('hollowing', or 'sagging'), he will be able to carry our weight more easily. If you are minded to do so, and have a child available, you can test this for yourself. Get down on your hands and knees, with your knees well up under your body and your back arched, and have the child sit on your back. Then, move your knees out more behind you, hollow your back and repeat.

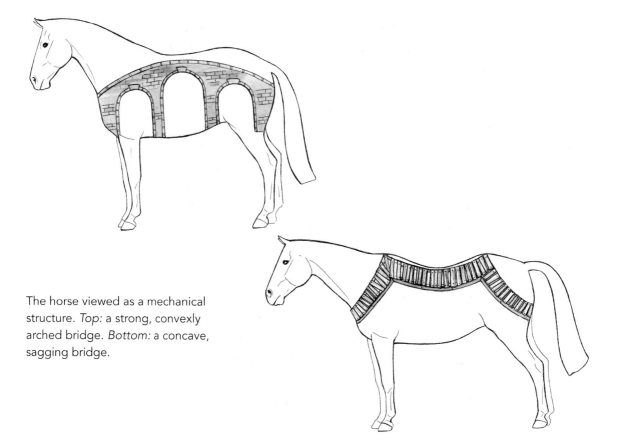

The horse viewed as a mechanical structure. *Top:* a strong, convexly arched bridge. *Bottom:* a concave, sagging bridge.

The difference will be obvious and there is no point in sending your osteopath's bill either to me or the publisher.

To go back to the horse's outline, it will be obvious that, in addition to the 'bridge' part, there is a long neck and a fairly big head attached to the front end. The horse is happy with this arrangement, since it lets him reach down to get some serious grazing done, but it does have the potential to complicate matters by affecting his overall balance. This issue is explained further on in the book (The Horse's Balance and What 'On the Forehand' Means) – but for the moment, let's concentrate on the fact that the vertebrae in the horse's neck are a continuation of his spine, and that there is a connection, via major ligaments, all the way from the top end of his neck to his pelvic region. This means that it is difficult for the horse to have an overall curvature of his neck which is at odds with the curvature of the rest of his spine. (See box below.) Put simply, whether his head is carried relatively low, or higher, if the curvature of his neck is basically convex, then the rest of his spine will be, too. If, on the other hand, his neck is basically concave ('hollow'), then that hollowness will be reflected in the main part of his spine. (Because of the inter-connection, these relationships work to a certain extent the other way round – the posture of the back being generally reflected in the neck.) So, if you want the horse to be able to carry you easily, you need to ride him in a way that encourages him to arch his neck and back, rather than hollowing them.

The next basic mechanical principle is that the horse is, or is intended to be, 'rear-engined'. His back end – his hindquarters and hind limbs – is designed to be the main source of propulsion, and he moves much more efficiently when he 'pushes' himself forward from behind than if he 'drags' himself along from in front. And there's more to this – we've already seen that there's a significant relationship between the

Difficult, but not altogether impossible. Horses, like people, can be forced into unnatural postures – in the horses' case by bad, coercive riding and the use of artificial gadgets. However, we are talking here of what is natural for the horse and I'm assuming that readers want to learn how to establish a co-operative partnership with the horse, not engage in weird acts of bondage.

main part of the horse's back and his head and neck, but there's another very important relationship between his back and his rear end. The mechanics of this are such that, when the horse flexes the joints in his hind limbs and steps forward actively ('underneath himself'), his back tends to round in a desirable way – and the more it does so, the more easily the hind limbs can 'step under', thus producing a positive snowball effect. Conversely, if the horse doesn't step forward actively with his hind limbs, this interaction doesn't take place. Furthermore, because of the link between his back and his hindquarters, if he is being ridden in a way that causes him to adopt a 'hollow' posture of his neck and back, this

Top: convex outlines of back and neck help the horse to carry weight and move efficiently. *Bottom:* concave outlines of back and neck reduce the horse's ability to carry weight and move efficiently.

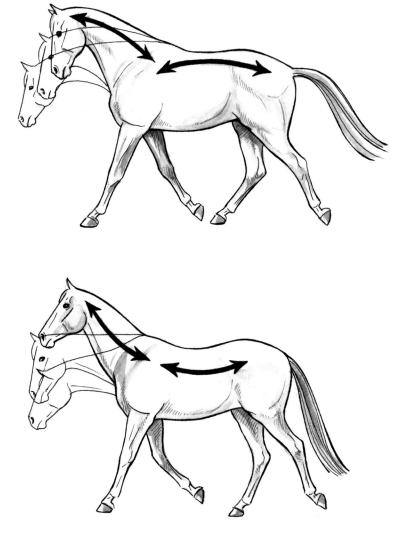

makes it *harder* for him to step forward actively with his hind legs and so it is difficult for them to move in a way that will help remedy the situation. Rather than being used in a way that will assist both carrying and propulsion, the horse's hind limbs will more or less 'trail' along behind him. So, being in a certain posture (or 'outline') doesn't only affect the horse's ability to carry you; it also affects how freely and efficiently he moves.

We can summarise these points by saying:

A *hollow* (concave) outline of his back and neck, with inactive 'trailing' hindquarters make it *hard* for the horse both to carry the rider and to move efficiently.

A *rounded* (convex) outline of his back and neck, coupled with 'active' hind limbs, which step forward 'underneath' his body, make it *easier* for the horse both to carry the rider and to move efficiently.

So, to get down to basics, you can either ride a horse like a saggy bridge with the handbrake on, or like a proudly arched bridge with the handbrake off.

In the sections that follow, we'll see that how you sit in the saddle and use the reins will have major influences on the horse's posture, for better or worse.

Posture, not Posing

If you have taken part in sports other than riding, you will realise the importance of stance and positioning. Examples are numerous, but let's look briefly at just a few. A golfer whose set-up and ball placement are faulty may struggle to hit the ball at all – and it will be a miracle if it ever goes in the intended direction. Tennis and squash players who cannot position themselves correctly have little control over their shots, and the same is true of batsmen at cricket. Those who participate in the martial arts will get flung around like litter in a hurricane if they do not learn how to stabilise their posture and control their bodies. Cyclists will be mechanically inefficient if they don't adjust their saddle and handlebars to put them in the optimum position for their physique. As for skiers and water skiers, until they establish reasonably correct posture for their sports, it's just a question of whether they spend more time on their face or their backside.

You may gather from the above that I want to stress the importance of good posture in riding – and you are absolutely right. One of the worst mistakes a newcomer to riding can make is to dismiss emphasis on posture as 'poncy posing', and one of the worst disservices an instructor can do to a pupil is to fail to correct serious errors of posture. Since posture is so important, I hope that your instructor will spend some time telling you how to sit on a horse and ironing out any serious errors. However, because this book is intended to be a companion to your practical instruction, I intend going into this matter in some detail, so that you can study the points raised at your leisure.

Faulty Postures

Before taking a look at the main elements of correct posture, let's look at the most common faulty positions that beginners put themselves in, to see *why* they will cause significant problems.

The most common faulty posture adapted by newcomers when they climb into the saddle is known by polite people as the 'chair seat', and by the rest of us as the 'lavatory seat'. Essentially, the rider's bum is parked against the back of the saddle (called the 'cantle'), and the legs are pushed forwards, with the lower legs and feet some way in front of the rider's body.

There is, I suppose, some justification for this in the first instance, because the rider is essentially sitting down on something and this posture does mimic the sort of posture we adopt when sitting (slouching) in a chair. (Those who frequent tall bar stools rather than low chairs may have a natural advantage in this respect.) However, as a basic position for riding, it has a number of major drawbacks:

1 In a correct posture, the rider's seat can be used as a subtle but effective means to send signals to the horse. It is the physical connection between the rider's weight and the horse's back and it can act to encourage or contain forward movement and to suggest changes of direction. In the chair seat, the altered relationship between the rider's seat and the horse's back does not allow this to be done effectively – the rider's bottom becomes just something to sit on.

2 Furthermore, sitting on the back of the saddle, rather than in its centre, places the rider just too far back to be 'with' the horse in motion – in terms of movement and balance the rider will always be what is called 'behind the movement'.

3 Because, in the chair seat, the rider is 'behind the movement' there will be a tendency for rein effects to have a 'backward' inclination. Beginners who may be more concerned about their ability to stop, rather than go, might initially view this as a good thing, but this is at best a short-term view. A learner driver may, at first, want to proceed with caution, but no one seriously thinks it's a good idea to drive everywhere with the handbrake on. Also, this 'back of the saddle pulling back on the reins posture' is certain to produce the undesirable 'hollow' outline just described in Very Basic Mechanics of the Horse.

4 In the chair seat, the rider's lower legs are positioned too far forward to allow them to be used effectively, either to encourage forward movement or to direct the horse.

5 This position, with everything from the hips downward stuck out in front of the upper body, is hopeless for absorbing the horse's natural movement. (When the body is in the correct posture, which we will discuss in due course, the musculature of the pelvic area can do a good job of this.) Therefore, particularly in trot, but also in canter, the rider will be bounced about willy-nilly and will instinctively try to establish some stability by gripping with the legs and/or hanging on to the reins. We have already seen (First Sensations in the Saddle) that this is a bad idea but, to reiterate briefly:
  - The clamped-on legs may well be interpreted by the horse as a crude signal to go faster.
  - Clamping on of legs is often accompanied by them being drawn up, causing possible loss of stirrups and a reduction in security.

So if, in this faulty posture, the rider reacts to the insecurity of being bounced around by gripping with the legs, this invites the following scenario – the horse may react by going faster and the rider's position may become increasingly insecure.

If the rider reacts to feelings of insecurity by hanging on by the *reins*, this *may* cause the horse to stop which – in the very short term – might seem like a good result. However, if every time the horse starts to go actively forward, the rider's actions cause him to stop, then the rider isn't going to get very far. On the other hand, horses don't like people hanging on to their reins – it's very uncomfortable for them and it interferes with their balance. So, rather than necessarily stopping, the horse may react by speeding up (in an attempt to 'escape' the discomfort), throwing his head around and becoming increasingly unbalanced. Again, this is not an ideal scenario for a rider who is feeling distinctly insecure.

If a rider reacts to feelings of instability both by clamping the legs on *and* hanging on by the reins, then the bottom line is that the horse will be receiving a conflicting set of crude 'go–stop' signals. Quite how he will interpret these is down to the individual horse, but it is a certainty that he will feel confused and uncomfortable. The *very best* that can be said about this situation is that it does not represent the clear communication that is a key to effective riding.

So, in summary, the chair seat is a posture that seriously compromises the rider's ability to give effective aids with any part of the body, and it offers little in terms of security.

Two examples of faulty posture. *Left:* the chair seat. *Below:* the foetal position.

However, there is a variation of the chair seat, sometimes adopted by newcomers, which is even worse, especially with regard to rider security. This is, essentially, a foetal position. The rider may adopt a similar lower body position to the chair seat but, whereas most chair seat riders will have their back more or less upright (or even lean back somewhat), the foetal rider will curl the upper body forward. There are two prevalent reasons for this:

Anxiety It is not uncommon for anxious or fearful people to adopt foetal postures in all sorts of circumstances. As I have explained, there should be no need for newcomers to riding to feel particularly worried, but individuals react differently to different situations and, if someone is anxious, then that is how they feel. A sympathetic and experienced instructor will no doubt find ways to alleviate this response, but they will also go on to correct this posture, because it is potentially dangerous and the last thing any beginner (let alone a worried one) wants, is an early fright or fall.

Misconception that what the rider perceives as leaning forward (in fact, this is curling up) will somehow make things easier for the horse. This misconception is common amongst people who are enthusiastic and sympathetic towards horses, but a good instructor will foster these attitudes whilst correcting the basic error. (There are *some circumstances* in which moving the upper body forward is appropriate, but this never entails curling up the spine. When and how to make adjustments to the normal posture are discussed in Part 6 – Out and About.)

The problem with the foetal posture is that it has all the disadvantages of the chair seat, plus one extra. I have mentioned that most chair seat riders tend to have their backs reasonably straight (or even to lean backwards) and the one saving grace of this is that, if the horse stumbles, or snatches at the reins, the rider's back will provide at least a modest bracing effect against the consequent forward pull. In the foetal position, however, the curved spine offers no resistance against these effects and the rider will inevitable succumb to them, experiencing a serious loss of balance forwards. (I have actually seen a rider, in this position at halt, pulled off over his horse's shoulder when the horse stretched down for a mouthful of grass.)

Before moving on to look at the elements and advantages of correct posture, there is one other faulty form that should be mentioned – the 'crotch' seat. This is actually pretty rare in beginners, but it is another posture based upon misconception and a newcomer to riding may possibly 'catch it' from a friend or family member who is an enthusiast – albeit a misguided one – for dressage. I mention this connection because this sort of position is most commonly adopted by people who think that it is an essential requirement of dressage to ride with the legs in an excessively 'long' position (hanging very far down the horse's sides), and positioned exaggeratedly far back. Now, for dressage riding, there are advantages in having long, supple legs, and experienced exponents, after many years in the saddle, will develop muscular suppleness and elasticity of the relevant tendons and ligaments that will enable them to sustain and use leg positions that the average rider would struggle to achieve. And that is the point. Since they cannot legitimately achieve such a position, some riders attempt to mimic it – and tipping forward onto their crotch is the only way in which they can get their legs anywhere near what they think of as the 'right position'. (This, in effect, is like a novice skier seeing a champion downhiller achieve an exceptional time on an Olympic run, and throwing himself of the top of the mountain because that's the only way he can match that speed!)

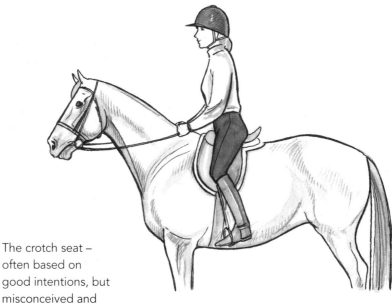

The crotch seat – often based on good intentions, but misconceived and ineffective.

Apart from being eye-wateringly uncomfortable, the tipped-on-the-crotch position is ineffective and precarious. It is ineffective because the backside, not being properly in the saddle, cannot give the seat aids mentioned earlier in a truly effective fashion and because, in order to maintain this position, the rider's legs have to 'hang on to' the horse's sides, so they are not really free to give either 'forward' or directional aids. It is precarious because, in tipping forward, the rider has sacrificed the stability provided by sitting fully on their seat and replaced it with a smaller, less stable 'fulcrum point'. In short, if the horse does anything that pulls the rider forward, the rider will be unable to resist.

Elements of Good Posture

So, having looked at incorrect postures, let's get on to look at what's right. The good news is that you can get a very close approximation of correct posture very easily, dismounted. This will give you a pretty good 'feel' of what it should be like and, if you've got a full-length mirror, you can get a visual image as well.

1 Stand 'to attention' – feet and legs together, upright, back straight, shoulders back a little, arms by your sides, fists lightly clenched, head up, looking straight ahead. Feel that you are standing erect, but without forcing the position and creating stiffness.

2 Move both feet outward, so that they are about shoulder-width apart (15 in or so). Don't splay your feet out – keep your toes pointing straight ahead.

3 Curl your head and neck down, just enough to see your toes. Try, so far as possible, to bend your neck only; keep the main part of your back straight – the idea is to be just able to see your toes, with minimal disturbance to your overall posture.

4 Keeping your back straight, allow your knees to flex forward until they have just obscured your sight of your toes – the best way to do this is to imagine that your bum is sinking down towards your heels. Once your toes have disappeared from view, carefully uncurl your neck so that your head is upright once more.

5 Keeping your elbows flexed, draw your forearms up and forward, until they are a few degrees short of horizontal to the ground, and move both fists inward, until they are about 5 in apart.

Practising to achieve correct posture dismounted.

Practise this procedure and get used to how the final position feels. One thing you should notice immediately is that it feels different from the descriptions given earlier of incorrect postures – there is no sense of unbalancing/tipping forward, which is a feature of the crotch seat, and you will note that your backside is not stuck out behind you, as it would be in the chair seat (if you check your side view in a mirror, you will see that your hips are pretty much vertically above your heels).

So, transposing this position into the saddle, what are its key features?

Your *backside* is in full contact with the lowest part of the saddle – which is where it should be. Your *upper body*, erect and vertically above your backside, drops your weight directly down into your seat, adding to security. Your *head* is erect, adding its weight effect to that of your upper body. (The head is heavy and, if it is inclined forward and down, this will tend to produce curvature further down the spine, destabilising the effectiveness of the upper body.) Your legs hang down freely, resting lightly against the horse's sides. The fact that you have two long, heavy limbs, one each side of the horse, hanging down below the level of your seat, further increases mechanical security. When your *feet* are placed into stirrups with leathers adjusted correctly for your physique, the flexion at knees and ankles will mimic that of the dismounted position just described, except that your toes will be slightly higher than your heels. As in the dismounted position, your toes should point pretty much straight ahead.

The basic and very important benefits of this position are:

- It maximises security.

- It permits your weight to remain stable, in the right place on the horse's back, thus promoting harmony and balance of the horse/rider unit.

- It places you in the position from which the aids can be applied to optimum effect. (We will look at the aids, and various aspects of communication with the horse, in due course.)

Correct posture in the saddle – secure and effective.

A Word About the Seat

In the earlier text describing the faulty chair seat, I mentioned that, when a rider is sitting correctly, the seat can be used as a subtle but highly effective means of sending signals to the horse. In fact, the more proficient a rider becomes, the more effective their seat aids, and the greater their relative importance.

However, in order for the seat aids to be effective, the seat itself *must* first be stabilised and pretty correct and, for most people, achieving this state takes a significant amount of time and practice. One factor is the time necessary for the muscles of the lower back, buttocks, pelvic area and upper thighs to take on riding 'tone', and for the associated ligaments to 'free up' a little. So, even for a newcomer who adopts a *technically* respectable posture from the beginning, developing a truly proficient seat must be considered a work in progress. If a rider with an unstable, incorrect position tries to give active seat aids, all that will happen is that the horse will become confused and unbalanced and the rider's own stability will be compromised. For these reasons, while there are some references throughout this book to basic functions of the seat, it doesn't go into great detail – not because the subject is unimportant, but because seat aids are *too important* to be rushed into and misapplied.

That said, the following is a very basic explanation of why the seat can be so effective, and what it can do, given so that you know what to aim for in the longer term.

The way in which the seat aids work relates to the rider's weight and the horse's sensitivity and balance. When correctly seated, a rider's weight is almost vertically over the horse's centre of motion (the mid-point along his spine between his forelegs and hind legs). The horse has a simple capacity, via his nervous system, to feel changes of pressure on his back and (notwithstanding the presence of a saddle), any slight shifts in the rider's actual seat are emphasised by the weight of the rider above it. Not only will the horse feel major changes in weight or pressure (such as an unbalanced rider thumping down in the saddle); he will also feel more minor changes, such as a rider contracting or relaxing muscles in the seat area, or placing more emphasis on one seat bone.

A proficient rider with a good posture can make subtle use of these facts to produce the following broad influences:

- Weight spread evenly over full seat (buttocks and upper thighs), upper body quietly erect. This represents the 'norm' – the seat is in 'quiet communication' with the horse, but not sending any specific signals.

- Slightly more weight on the buttocks and less on the upper thighs and what is commonly referred to as slight bracing of the lower back. (The term 'braced back' is sometimes misinterpreted as meaning a markedly stiffened or hollow back, which are not what is required – they promote tension in both rider and horse and reduce the 'shock absorber' effect of the rider's seat. In order to achieve the desired effect, it may help to think of making a little extra effort to sit erect, moving the shoulder blades slightly closer together and pushing the lower back *fractionally* forward.) This is a 'driving' seat; used together with pressure from the legs and a slight softening of the rein contact, it encourages extra forward movement; used together with 'quiet' legs and gently restraining hands, it produces a 'steadying' effect.

This is probably the seat effect most open to being misunderstood and misused, with riders leaning back and thrusting with the rear of the seat. The main effects of this are that the rider comes 'behind the movement' (and may inadvertently harden the rein contact at the same time), and the horse 'hollows' his back away from the grinding pressure of the seat).

- Slightly less weight on the buttocks and more on the thighs; upper body inclined (not curled) very slightly forward. This is the 'light seat', used to encourage a horse (perhaps a younger animal, or one who tends to hollow his back) to round his back and engage his hind legs. It also mimics the posture of the 'rising' phase of rising trot (see Rising Trot) and is an embryonic form of the 'poised position' used with shortened stirrup leathers when riding at speed in the open (see Cantering in the Open).

- More weight on one seat bone. This is sometimes called a loaded seat aid and it is used in turns and lateral movements. It uses the horse's instinct to remain in balance by adjusting his own posture and movement to take account of any change in weight distribution on his back.

This requires subtle control of posture; the rider's upper body should remain upright, with no leaning over. You can practise this effect on a firm stool – feel the difference between sitting erect and pressing down with one seat bone as opposed to leaning over.

As implied earlier in this section, the most constructive way a novice rider can set about learning to use the seat is, in the first instance, to work on developing good posture. In practice, riders who do this, whilst carrying out the various exercises suggested by a good instructor, may find they are beginning to make constructive use of the seat almost unconsciously – a much better basis for progress than the uncoordinated thrusting and leaning that may arise from trying too hard, too soon.

Using Your Legs

The rider's legs are used to encourage the horse to go forwards, either with more energy or into a different gait, and to help direct him. How you use them is very important. Earlier, when discussing how you could practise the elements of good riding posture on the ground (see Posture, not Posing), I mentioned that your toes should point pretty much straight forward. If you have your toes turned outwards and your heels up, not only will you look like a penguin with piles, but your legs will follow the lead of your feet and also turn outwards away from the horse. This will make you less secure and more likely to bounce around in the saddle – which won't help your horse. Also, it will mean that the only signals you can give (they won't really be aids) will be by swinging your lower legs away from the horse and kicking with your heels – and while they're swinging away from the horse, your legs can't be in communication with him so, at that point, they can't, for instance, help keep him straight or turn through a corner.

Incorrect leg position – toes down, heels up and legs turned away from the horse – insecure and ineffective.

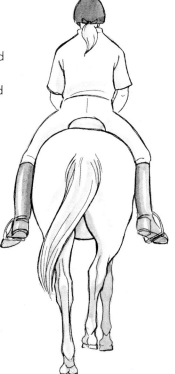

To make your leg aids effective, think about keeping your toes pointing pretty much forwards, and having your heels *a little* lower than your toes. A couple of points on these issues:

1 Toes pointing pretty much forward is actually a *more natural* position than the splay-footed posture. If you sit astride a push-bike or a motor-bike, it is highly unlikely that you will feel inclined to splay your feet out and, if you sit down casually on a chair, while your toes probably won't point directly forward, it is also unlikely that they will splay out sideways. Riders who turn their toes out to a marked degree do so either in an erroneous attempt to enhance security ('gripping' with the lower calves) or in order to give 'aids' with their heels. In fact, because this 'toes out' posture turns most of the upper legs away from the horse, this gripping actually *reduces* security (and the constant squeezing from the heels doesn't impress the horse) and the 'aids' given this way are generally ineffective, for reasons that will be explained shortly. So, since the 'toes out' posture is more about mental misconceptions than physical difficulty, it is a habit best avoided.

2 Although the heels should be a *little* lower than the toes, don't *force* them down: doing so will stiffen your ankle joints and produce a lot of tension in your calves – and probably further up the legs and in the seat as well. It may help to imagine that your legs are made of lead, which is melting down into your boots, because this image is about *allowing* the weight of your legs down into your ankles (and the stirrups) rather than about *forcing* a leg position.

When you get your lower legs into the correct 'toes forward, heels slightly down' position, your calf muscles will be bulging gently against the horse's sides, and you will only have to close your legs inwards to give quite a firm signal. Also, because your lower legs are close to your horse's sides, your knees and thighs will follow that position and this will help you to sit securely and still.

An important point about giving aids for forward movement with your legs is knowing when to give them and when to stop doing so. This applies to other aids as well, but perhaps more to leg aids than any others. Suppose you give the horse a leg aid to go into trot. Perhaps he's a bit lazy, or slow to respond, so the aid is quite a strong one. But then he goes; he's

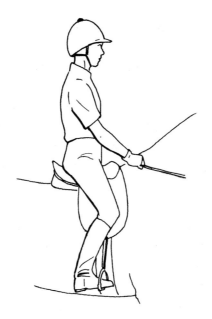

Correct lower leg position – toes forward and slightly higher than heel, leg resting against horse's side.

trotting quite actively – so what do you do now? The answer is keep your legs resting quietly against his sides, think about the rhythm of the trot and be prepared to give another signal as soon *as you feel him beginning to flag* (see A Stitch in Time). If, on the other hand, you keep kicking him 'in case he thinks about slowing down' (or just mindlessly), then you are telling him to do something he's already doing. If someone did that to you, you would think they were a real pain, and you'd stop paying attention – and the same thing happens with horses. Ridden like this, they become what is called 'dead to the leg'. So, always think about the signals you are giving and don't 'nag' unnecessarily.

Using your legs to give directional aids is discussed in Showing, not Steering, Circling and Two Lateral Exercises.

Rein Contact

Rein contact is, essentially, one of the most basic concepts in riding, but really understanding its significance, controlling it and interpreting signals received from it is something that many riders struggle to grasp. Because it is quite literally a matter of 'feel' (what you can feel in your hands), fully understanding and interpreting 'contact' is something that needs to be developed over time but, as with certain other aspects of riding, understanding *why* it is so important is the first incentive for wanting to learn about it.

The reins themselves are simply strips of leather (or other material) which provide a connection between the rider's hands and the horse's mouth. As we saw earlier (First Sensations in the Saddle) they are *not* for holding on by; they exist to allow the rider to communicate directly with the horse's front end, to help control and direct the energy that the horse produces from his rear end. Learning how to do this subtly, to optimum effect, is a continuing process; what we are talking about at this stage is establishing a starting point.

Rein contact, at the most fundamental level, means that there is sufficient tension in the reins for the rider's hands at one end, and the horse's mouth at the other, to be able to feel one another – it is this that provides the basis for communication.

If there is no tension on the reins (they are completely slack), there can be no positive communication through them. This is a bit like you and a friend both having telephones with the receivers in their cradles: the phones work all right, but there will be no communication between them until one of you picks up the receiver and dials, and the other one picks up the receiver and answers. (See also box below.)

If there is a lot of tension in the reins, this will influence the action of the bit in the horse's mouth; whatever its pattern, one way or another it will increase pressure on the mouth significantly. Now, while it is the *purpose* of a bit to send signals to the horse via varying degrees of sensation, the pressure applied should usually be as little as is necessary to obtain the desired response. Unless it has been damaged by very bad riding, a horse's mouth is highly sensitive and the aim is to get a willing response to light rein aids. Such aids will keep the horse happy and

This slack rein is not inevitably 'wrong' – an experienced rider, on a well-schooled horse who has been working hard, may sometimes allow the horse to walk for a while on loose reins to let him stretch the muscles of his neck and back and relax. However, even for a truly experienced partnership, it remains a fact that, while the reins are slack, there is no active communication down them.

Top left: acceptable, light but evident rein contact. *Above right:* rider has unintentionally let reins go slack (no contact). *Right:* heavy rein contact – rider 'hanging on' causing discomfort and resistance in the horse.

co-operative, which is good of itself, and – from a pragmatic viewpoint – if you are sitting on top of a half-ton animal, it is reassuring to know that he is likely to slow down or stop when asked *nicely*. However, if the horse's mouth is subjected to strong pressure – especially if this is protracted – the horse will inevitably be uncomfortable, and he will react in various ways – all of them undesirable. The two most obvious reactions are:

1 He will 'resist' (struggle against) the discomfort of the bit. A rider who interprets this simply as 'fighting/pulling back', and responds by taking an even stronger hold on the reins, is simply instigating a downward spiral (and who needs a tug of war with a creature six times their weight?).

2 Because of the discomfort in his mouth, he will be reluctant to move smoothly and freely forward, so the quality of any forward movement will be seriously compromised.

So, in all normal circumstances, what is needed is a rein contact that is sufficient to allow active communication with the horse, but which is light enough to allow him to go forward comfortably in the way that the rider desires. How is this achieved? Well, the key here is to go back to the idea that the reins are just strips of leather, with the rider's hands at one end and the bit (in the horse's mouth) at another. Simply speaking, we could say that, whatever sensations occur at one end of the rein will be felt at the other: that what the rider feels in the hands, the horse feels in his mouth, and vice versa. In practice, because of the mechanical action of most types of bit, sensations are likely to be heightened to some degree at the horse's end – so we can say that, whatever the rider feels at one end of the reins, the horse will feel at the other (but a little more so.) So, for a 'starting point', workable contact, you need a feeling in your hands that tells you there's something at the other end of the reins you are in communication with – and the basic message you are receiving should be telling you that the horse is happy with the degree of contact. The evidence for this is the feeling that he is doing what is called 'accepting the contact' – he is maintaining a light, but distinct pressure on the bit, neither pulling against the reins, nor trying to arch his neck excessively and tuck his head into his chest to avoid the contact (actions known as 'overbending' and 'going behind the bit'). See box on page 50.

And now to the crux of the matter – a basic *monitoring* of the contact and any changes to it, which is the starting point for developing the 'feel' that will be so important to your progress as a rider.

If you start off with a distinct but 'acceptable' contact, and the feeling in your hands changes, this can only be for one of two reasons: either you have changed the amount of tension on the reins, or the horse has. Now it might be that you have done so, either from choice or by accident, so we'll look at these possibilities first.

These actions are not to be confused with the posture of highly-trained horses, such as those of the famous Spanish Riding School of Vienna, who will be seen in pictures to be moving with proudly arched necks and perpendicular faces. A highly trained horse, taking and responding to a very light rein contact, is completely different from an uncomfortable horse trying to avoid the contact. We could make an analogy with someone holding a fine bone china cup lightly because it is a delicate rarity, as compared to someone holding a tin cup gingerly because the hot liquid in it is burning their fingers.

The horse on the *left* is uncomfortable and is trying to avoid contact with the bit ('overbent'); the horse on the *right* has a proudly arched neck and is taking a light contact – a consequence of excellent balance. These two postures indicate completely different ways of going.

If you have *chosen* to change the tension on the reins, this presupposes that you didn't think the previous contact was appropriate, so you will know *why* you have done it. (At an early stage, if your instructor thinks you made the wrong decision, he or she should tell you why.)

If you have changed the tension *by accident*, this tells you one of two basic things:

1 You have lost your balance/position in some way, resulting in more or less tension on the reins. This is an example of how involuntary movements on the rider's part send unintended signals to the horse, and the basic remedy for changes of contact of this sort lies in attention to maintaining good posture and balance.

2 If the contact has been accidentally reduced or lost, this means that you have allowed one or both reins to slip through your fingers. Now, although some riding school reins are undesirably thin, and although reins can get a bit slippery when wet (one good reason for wearing gloves), it is not that technically difficult to hold on to a rein. The main reason why novice riders lose rein contact involuntarily (and it is a common error) is simply lack of attention to detail. *They just let them slip through their fingers.* The key to avoiding this lies not in holding the reins in a vice-like grip (which will tense up your forearms and send a hard, unyielding feeling down the reins), but simply on concentrating on what you are feeling in your hands.

There is also a third possibility relating to accidental changes of contact, which can relate in part to either or both of the above, but may also have other causes. This is that the contact, which started out pretty much equal in both reins, has become uneven: there is considerably more contact on one rein than the other. As you progress with your riding, there will be times when your instructor explains that, for a specific purpose, you should have a slightly different degree of contact on one rein than the other. However, at an early stage, when you are carrying out very basic exercises, the contact should usually feel pretty much the same in both hands. If it feels markedly different, you should glance at your hands to see what is going on. Is one hand higher than the other, or more forward or back? This sort of positioning can creep in unnoticed by the rider (but not the horse) through unintentional shifts of posture or, quite commonly, because a rider is predominantly left- or right-handed (the dominant hand takes a stronger contact, and is often carried higher, than the other one). While the unintentional shifts of posture should be corrected readily by appropriate advice from your instructor, the 'dominant hand' issue can be an insidious part of anyone's make-up, and this may require frequent attention over a considerable period before the unconscious but ingrained habit is broken. However, if we revert to the topic of 'feel', a constant monitoring of what can be felt in the hands will help alert 'dominant-handed' riders, as well as others whose contact has changed unwittingly, to any lapses, which should be corrected by evening it up.

(A common fault is to have a considerably stronger contact with the inside hand than the outside hand on turns. This happens because riders try to pull a horse through a turn – for example, to the right, by pulling back on the right rein.) The reason why this is a serious mistake is explained in more detail in Showing, not Steering.)

Holding one hand higher than the other (*left*) is a fault that can creep in unnoticed by the rider, but the effect will be noticed by the horse. Level hands (*right*) will help to ensure a more even contact in both reins.

If the contact has changed, and it is not you who has changed it, then it must be down to the horse. Again, his actions will have either decreased or increased it. *Monitoring cases where this had happened, analysing why and responding accordingly is one of the major building blocks of becoming an active, thinking rider.*

With most riding school horses, *decreased* contact is likely to be associated with loss of activity on the horse's part (the horse is no longer stepping forward 'into' your hands. A good instructor should pick up on the reason and suggest a correction but, generally, this will entail using your leg aids to send the horse forward more actively ('riding him forward into your hands'). In due course, you will learn to relate this to other signals that the horse is losing his activity (see A Stitch in Time...) and thus make your own corrections at an early stage.

If the horse *increases* the contact, he will do so in one of three basic ways:

1 By 'leaning on the bit'.

2 By 'pulling'.

3 By raising his head, or 'going above the bit'.

Again, a good instructor should notice what has happened and suggest a correction but, very briefly:

'Leaning on the bit' can sometimes have a specific cause, such as a horse wanting to snatch a mouthful of grass, or to stretch his neck in order to sneeze or cough. The former is bad manners and the correction is to send him forwards with strong leg aids (not to try to pull him up with your hands; a tug of war that may pull muscles in your arms or back – see also Three Tips, in Riding Out). In the latter case, it is entirely correct to allow the horse longer reins for a moment of two, so that he can 'clear his tubes' and make himself comfortable.

In most cases, however, leaning on the bit signifies some lack of balance on the horse's part, so that too much weight is placed on his front end (called 'going on the forehand'). This, and what to do about it, is discussed in more detail in The Horse's Balance and What 'On the Forehand' Means – for the time being, we can just recognise that the heavy sensation in the hands indicates that something in the horse's way of going requires attention.

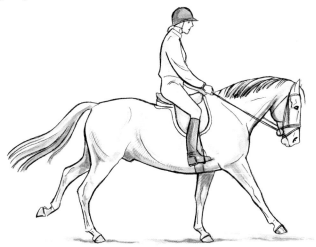

A constant heavy sensation in your hands indicates that the horse is 'leaning on the bit' – most probably because his balance is faulty.

Pulling is basically something a horse does if he wants to go faster than his rider; he more or less fights the restraint of the reins. Few riding school horses are renowned for wanting to go faster than duty requires (and any who do so habitually are not suitable for novice riders), but occasionally a horse may think that rushing round to the rear of the ride will give him a longer time to rest, or he may feel a sudden urge to bite the bum of the horse in front.

A pulling horse feels strong in your hands because he wants to hurry along faster than you want him to go.

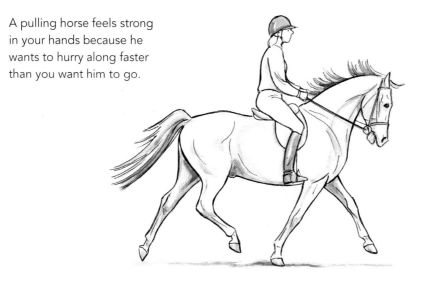

The key to controlling a pulling horse lies not in actively pulling back, but in keeping the hands and forearms still (in passive resistance) and maintaining a good, firm seat in the saddle, and an upright posture. In that way, resistance comes from the big muscles of your seat and back, rather than just from your hands. (This is a bit like those party tricks where you make yourself 'heavy' or 'light', and it also relates to the postures adopted by exponents of martial arts.) When a horse responds to this resistance by ceasing to pull, it is important to lighten the contact slightly, so that he is rewarded for his compliance.

(The section on Cantering in the Open contains more advice on controlling horses who pull or become rather keen when ridden at speed outdoors.)

Going above the bit describes a horse who raises his head abnormally high in an attempt to avoid the rein contact. In doing so, he produces a 'hollow' outline in his neck (and back) which, as we saw earlier, is undesirable in terms of efficient movement. Horses may take on this outline for a variety of reasons connected with discomfort (toothache, pain from the bit, back problems, ill-fitting saddle, etc.) but, assuming that the school keeps a check on the horse's welfare, the most likely reason for a horse to do it is rider-related. If it happens, check your position in the saddle, ask yourself whether *your* basic rein contact is light and friendly, and whether you are riding the horse actively forwards into this contact.

A horse who is 'above the bit' carries his head abnormally high; there can be various reasons for this but, if it happens, you should always check your position and rein contact.

Notes on Rein Contact

1 Length of rein is *not the same* as degree of contact. The degree of contact is about the *tension* on the reins. It is entirely possible to have short reins but no contact, or quite long reins and a heavy contact. However, some instructors fall into the habit of equating rein length with degree of contact and they may tell a pupil to 'shorten your reins' when what they mean essentially is 'take up a contact' (that has been lost). Of course, it is perfectly correct for an instructor to tell a pupil to shorten their reins if these have become unmanageably long – but it is important to understand the distinction between these situations.

2 When a horse moves in different gaits, he adapts his physical outline in subtle ways, according to the gait. To give simple examples, when a horse is walking he will move his head and neck more than when he is trotting (and when he canters and gallops, he will move them in quite a complex cyclical way). If you are to maintain a consistent, light rein contact in the various gaits, it is important to learn how to move your hands subtly *in accord with* the movement of the horse's head, so that the degree of contact remains consistent. I would emphasise that this is something that comes gradually, with practice and increased 'feel', but it will not develop at all if you are not, in the first instance, aware of the basic concept of 'contact'.

Length of rein is not the same as degree of contact. It is possible to have short reins but no contact (*top*) or long reins and a heavy contact (*bottom*).

A General Note About the Aids and Communication

Anyone who is keen to learn how to do anything well will look for the most precise and accurate explanation of how to proceed. The desire to learn definitive techniques that produce optimum results in all circumstances is entirely sensible.

However, life is not always quite that simple. In riding, a major element is communication with horses, and horses are living creatures, all of whom differ slightly in their individual characteristics. This is why it is so important to understand the basic *principles* of riding – because they are constant, whereas the precise details of *practice* may be influenced by a wide range of variables. Realistically, this observation applies to many processes – including those that might be thought of as entirely mechanical (i.e. 'pull this lever, press that button…'). Take, for example, a car with a manual gearbox. In any such car the clutch, gear lever, brake and accelerator all have the same basic functions but, from car to car they vary in aspects such as clutch biting point, number of gears, effectiveness with which brakes function, rate of acceleration (and underlying power of the engine). So, for example, the principle in every manual car is that you depress the clutch before you change gear, then release it, but the precise details of how (and when) you change gear *for maximum smoothness and efficiency* vary from one car to another. And that's with a mechanical vehicle – there are far more potential variations from horse to horse, rooted in factors such as temperament, sensitivity, physique, athleticism and level of training.

Now, I don't want to overstate the case here and I should make it clear that *all* horses deemed suitable for beginners should be of such character, temperament and level of training that they will neither ignore, nor react violently or bizarrely to aids applied with even modest degrees of competence. Indeed, there are some wise old school horses who make great efforts to interpret and comply with signals which, in their terms, must seem the most rudimentary 'pidgin English'. However, it is the case that all horses are individuals and one thing you will learn early on is that the precise way in which you gave the aids to one horse may not have *exactly* the same result on another. This might, in the early stages, be confusing and even a little dispiriting, but part of the challenge of riding lies in figuring out how to communicate effectively with different horses – and the long-term effect will be to improve your rider's 'vocabulary'.

Any good instructor will be aware of this issue, and should be prepared to explain how different horses may require slightly different approaches.

Why They're Called Aids

The signals riders give to their horses are traditionally called 'aids' – the really old English term was 'helps' – and there's an important clue here. Certainly, we send signals to the horse to *tell* him what we want him to do, but really good signals actually *help* him to respond. Of course, as a novice, you will sometimes send the horse confusing signals – perhaps because you're a bit out of balance or you've got the timing wrong – that is pretty much inevitable. The important thing is that you understand the bottom line. If you give an employee, or your child, a garbled, confused instruction, it's unfair to blame them if they misunderstand. If your signals to a horse confuse and unbalance him, you can't blame him if he doesn't make a smooth turn or transition – and, in these circumstances, you can't really call the signals *aids*. So, at times when a horse doesn't do exactly what you wanted, *consider the possibility* that you had something to do with this! And remember, the *aim* is to ask the horse in a way that will help him to respond.

The very important consideration of your own security aside, having this aim in mind is one of the biggest motivations for developing good posture and balance in the saddle. If you are unstable, your involuntary shifts of weight will cause the horse to readjust his own balance to keep the horse/rider unit in balance; if you are 'hanging on' with gripping legs and hands, these will send him involuntary, confusing signals. *The fact that these signals are sent unintentionally doesn't mean that the horse won't receive them* – but these signals are hindrances, not helps.

Bossing or Communicating?

There is a common misconception amongst beginners that the reason why the instructor can get the horse to do something correctly, whereas they themselves struggle, is that the horse 'knows the instructor is the boss'. Of course, there is an important element of truth here, insofar as it is the rider who should be in control. However, referring back to the previous section (Why They're Called Aids) the main point is that the instructor is giving *aids* that the horse can interpret clearly, whereas the beginner may be sending *signals* that are ineffective and/or confusing. It is very important that novice riders aim to achieve *clearer communication*, rather than getting into a mindset of trying to dominate the horse. For a graphic illustration of this, watch a video of a really top dressage partner-ship, or a display by the Spanish Riding School. The riders will *appear* to be doing very little (and what they can be seen to be doing will have a light touch), while the horses will be doing all sorts of complex move-ments, apparently almost of their own volition. This is effective com-munication in action.

A Stitch in Time...

One of the big differences between experienced riders and most novices is that the former subconsciously monitor what the horse is doing and correct him *as soon as they feel* he is about to make some change of his own accord. For the expert rider, these corrections will include the most subtle adjustments to almost anything that is not exactly as they require it. This is one reason why experts *appear* to be doing so little: because they correct minor imperfections as soon as they notice them, they rarely have to make big efforts to correct obvious problems.

While, as a beginner rider, you cannot expect to have expert levels of perception and skill, the *concept* of making corrections as early as possible is something that is very important to take on board, and there is no reason why you cannot start working on this from a very early stage. You may, in fact, already have heightened powers of perception that have been developed in different situations. If you have young children, you will doubtless have developed a hypersensitive 'radar' system, acutely tuned to what they are doing, or about to do, even if you can only glimpse them out of the corner of one eye. If you are a driver you will know that, even on quiet roads, while there may be times when you're not doing much mechanically (not giving the car many 'aids'), it's important that you are constantly monitoring what's going on around you: checking the mirror, watching out for people pulling out of driveways, children or animals running out into the road, the glare of headlights on the hedgerow that tell you there's another vehicle coming towards you round a blind bend. Taking the same mindset into the saddle is a keystone to effective riding – constantly feeling and thinking how your horse is moving and responding is the basis of effective communication and, in mental terms, is the key difference between being a rider, as opposed to a passenger.

In the early stages of riding the first, most obvious use of perception, concerns times when the horse speeds up or slows down of his own accord. I've said 'of his own accord' here because there may be times when he changes speed because you have sent him involuntary signals to do so. If your heels give him an unintentional dig in the ribs, he is likely to respond by speeding up; if you get unbalanced and hang on to the reins, he is likely to slow down. However, these issues are distinct from the one we are discussing at present.

So, why might the horse speed up or slow down of his own accord? Well, in the great scheme of things, there could be a number of reasons, but let's take some simple scenarios from an early class lesson. Let's assume that you have reached the stage of trotting, and there's an exercise for individuals to trot on at intervals to take the rear of the ride. If your horse has one of his particular pals in front of him (or if he thinks that, the sooner he reaches the rear of the ride, the sooner he can have a doss), he may speed up on the way round the school. If, on the other hand, he had been 'getting a tow' from the horse in front (keeping up with that horse as a result of herd instinct – see also Don't Take a 'Tow') and he suddenly finds himself at the front of the ride, he may decide that natural leadership is not his thing, and slow down.

If you want to become an active rider, it is very important, from an early stage, to develop the *intention* to be in control of the horse's speed. (At a later stage, this will be about more than just speed, but this is a starting point.) If you are going to exercise this control then, first, you must be fully aware of his speed at any given moment, and second, you must be able to judge whether it is what you require.

If you are working as part of a 'ride' (all together), you can get some idea of whether you are going too fast or too slow by reference to the other riders. However, this can be misleading because it is at least possible that *they* may be going at the wrong speed too! Also, in due course, you will want to develop your own judgement about such matters.

One way in which you can begin to do this is by tuning in to the rhythm of the horse's movement. This is something even very inexperienced riders can do if they think about what is happening. For example, even someone who dances like a dad at a wedding has enough sense of rhythm to feel and count the 1,2,1,2 rhythm of a horse trotting beneath them. (For walk, the count should be a measured, regular 1,2,3,4 and for canter a repeated 1,2,3 beat.) At an early stage, you may not be in a position to judge whether the rhythm is the ideal one for this horse at this gait – just as you might not be able to judge whether a piece of music you are hearing for the first time is being played a little slower or faster than the composer intended. However, once you have tuned in to the rhythm in which the horse is moving, you will be able to pick up on any *changes* to it. If it slows down, or speeds up, you will be instantly aware of the change and in a position to do something about it. If you feel the rhythm dropping off a little, use your legs to ask the horse for more energy; a minor correction and you're back on rhythm. Isn't that better than waiting until the horse slumped into the kind of walk he'd do going to his own funeral, and then giving him a great kick to try to get him going again?

If you feel the rhythm quickening, sit still and upright in the saddle for a moment, and increase the rein contact slightly by closing your hands more firmly round the reins, until you feel the rhythm steadying, then ease off and allow the horse to move freely forwards in the steadier rhythm. See also the box below.

If you make a point of listening to the rhythm of the horse's movement you will find, through practice, that, in addition to picking up changes you *can* judge whether or not the *basic* rhythm is satisfactory. This will help you become much more proactive as a rider since you will automatically begin to *tell* the horse how you want him to move, rather than just accepting whatever movement he gives you.

As you become tuned in to the idea of monitoring unwanted changes in the horse's way of going, you will find that this will start to include things such as rein contact, straightness and balance – then you are on your way to riding like the experts do – making corrections almost before anyone else notices.

In addition to monitoring rhythm, there is another exercise some instructors use, which also has the aim of making pupils more aware of what is happening underneath them. This is to get them to count the number of strides the horse takes along two parallel sides of the school. The reasoning behind this is simple – if the horse is moving in a regular fashion, then (provided that the school is on level ground) the number of strides should be the same for both sides. If it is not, then the horse's *stride length* is not constant. At a more advanced level, riders will sometimes carry out exercises in which they *ask* the horse to change length of stride but, where this is not the case, any change means that things are happening beneath the saddle that the rider has neither asked for, nor corrected.

Timing Aids

To have the desired effect, the aids must be given at the right time and, where appropriate, in the correct order.

Let's make a couple of analogies with car driving. If you want to make a right turn in your car, it is important that you turn the steering wheel at the correct moment, and the right amount, otherwise you may knock over the post box on the pavement, or end up inside a furniture lorry. If you have to negotiate a busy roundabout, then the appropriate combinations of braking, gear changing, signalling and steering are essential, if you are not to end up in hospital and the courts, while your car heads off for the scrapyard. This, mind you, is in a mechanical vehicle which – if your mechanic is not a total cowboy – can be pretty much guaranteed to do what you ask.

In riding, there is a classical principle relating to the aids: PREPARE, ASK, ALLOW. As just noted, even in your car, which is incapable of thought, preparation can be an issue. A horse, far from being a mindless mechanism, is a sentient creature. Whilst trotting round the school, although he *should* be listening to you, his rider, it is possible that his mind is on his dinner, or his mates in the field, or he may just be assuming that he's supposed to keep going round and round the track, like he's been doing for the last five minutes. So, he may not have his attention fully on you and (especially if that is the case) he may not be in particularly good balance. If, while he is in this condition, you ask him suddenly to do something, his response will leave something to be desired. If you ask him to turn, it will be late and unbalanced; he will lose some of whatever activity he had, and he will probably wander off the required line. If you ask him for a downward transition, he will probably fall into it, like a sack of spuds that's been shot by a stun gun. If you ask him for an upward transition, he will either be startled into 'running' into it, or give you a slovenly 'token gesture', like a teenager asked to help with the washing up. ('What do you mean this isn't a proper trot? Look, I'm moving my feet in diagonal pairs…sort of. You're so unfair…').

So, the first part of timing the aids concerns preparation. This, to some extent, is ongoing. The more attentive you keep the horse at all times, the less effort you will need to gain his attention for a specific purpose (see also A Stitch in Time…) However, just as you have to think ahead to manoeuvre a car, so it is with a horse. Even if he is fully attentive, he is still a big, long animal: he will need a moment to respond to your aids. If you ask him to halt, he can't freeze instantaneously in mid-stride – and he can't make sudden, inexplicable changes of direction like a camera-shy UFO.

The precise amount of reaction time a horse will require will depend on many factors, including his individual sensitivity, his level of activity, his physique, his balance and what he is being asked to do. However, by way of basic guidance, if you intend to halt (from walk) at a specific school marker (see Geography and Geometry), you will need to start *asking* for the halt at least a horse's length *before* the marker, so you will need to have finished any preparation before this. Similarly, if you want to ride a turn (say a 90 degree turn across the school from the E marker, then you will need to be *starting* the turn several metres *before* the marker so, again, your preparation must be completed before that point. (There

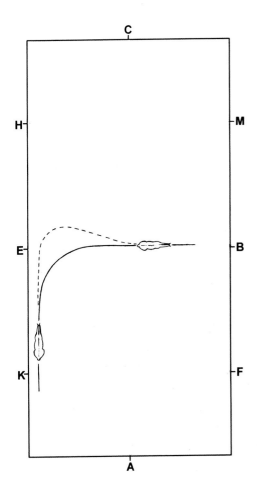

Correct (*solid line*) and incorrect ways (*dotted line*) to turn across the centre of the school. They represent proper preparation and lack of preparation respectively.

is a slight difference with upward transitions – from a 'slower' gait to a 'faster' one in that, as your skill increases, you will be able to ask for the transition *almost* where you want it to take place. However, in order to achieve such an accurate transition, your *preparation* must be completed beforehand.)

So, we can see that there is a close relationship between the 'prepare' and 'ask' phases of giving the aids. This is also true of the 'asking' and 'allowing' phases: we must 'ask' in a way that *allows* the horse to respond easily and promptly. It is no good asking one of your children to take a letter to the post box and promptly locking the front door, and it is no good asking a horse to go from walk to trot and promptly socking him in the mouth with the bit. We must always monitor our own actions to check that they are helping, not hindering the horse. There is a big difference between the horse who *won't* comply and the horse whose attempts at compliance are being *disrupted or prevented* by the rider.

Showing, not Steering

This section summarises many of the points made in Part 2 of this book by combining some practical uses of the 'mechanical' aids with the principle that thoughtful, effective aids are rarely 'big' aids.

A major mistake made by many novice riders is that they make big, obvious uses of the reins in their efforts to 'steer' the horse. One reason for this can be that their rein contact (see the section on that subject) is non-existent – and because their reins are long and slack they have to move their hands and forearms a good deal before any signal arrives at the horse's end of the reins. However, even if their length of rein and the contact are adequate, many people make too much (incorrect) use of the reins in their attempts to 'steer' the horse.

Try this experiment: walk, naturally in a small circle, say about 9 ft in diameter, and part-way round it become aware of your head and neck. You will find that your head is *very slightly* turned in the direction of the circle – but the inclination will be *very slight* – your head will not be screwed round to the inside. Like you, the horse (who will be going in much bigger circles than the size just mentioned) needs only a very modest directing of his head to go where you want him to go, *provided that the rest of his body is also channelled in that direction.* So, the proper directional role of the reins is simply to give the horse a subtle indication of the direction to look in ('showing' him the way); the main directional aids come from the correct use of the rider's legs (and, as the rider's skills develop, from subtle redistribution of weight). We will look further at these directional aids in a minute, but first let's focus on another serious but common error in how the rein aids are applied.

A major fault is trying to give directional aids on the reins by pulling back on them – for instance, trying to turn the horse left by pulling on the left rein. This might seem, at first sight, a logical thing to do, but a little more thought will show that it is, in fact, wildly *illogical*:

- In the first instance, increased backward pressure on the rein (and thus the bit) gives a crude signal to the horse to slow down or stop. Since going round a corner is mechanically more difficult for a horse than going in a straight line, the chances are that the horse's tendency will be to lose forward impulse through a corner so, if you want to retain it, the last thing you want to do is give him a signal to slow down.

Correct (*left*) and incorrect (*right*) ways to turn a horse. In the left-hand picture, the rider is giving the horse a subtle indication with the rein to look a little to his left – the main directional aids will come from the rider's legs and position. In the right-hand picture, the rider is pulling the left rein out and back – this is not only unnecessary, it will actually make it harder for the horse to turn correctly and fluently.

• Second, a backward pull on the inside of the horse's mouth will cause him to draw his head back and 'scrunch up' his neck on that side. In an attempt to realign his back end with his front end (an instinctive reaction), he will swing his hindquarters out in the other direction (in our example, to the right) in a horsy version of a rear wheel skid. This will mean that his 'rear wheel drive' is no longer aligned behind his front end and, just as with a motorised vehicle, the ability to control and direct the power is lost.

In order to avoid these problems, what is needed is a set of aids that will channel the *whole horse* smoothly through the turn, in a way that will encourage him to keep up his level of activity. The role of the hands/reins in this, while important, is minor. All that is required of the inside hand, even on a 90 degree turn, is to *indicate* the required direction of travel. In practice, this inside rein aid is achieved by moving your inside hand *forward* and out a little. Sitting in a chair, hold your hands and arms as if you were holding the reins: elbows by your sides, hands 4 to 5 inches apart. Now, keeping your elbows at your sides, simply allow whichever arm you choose as your 'inside' one to pivot outward a little from the elbow joint. You will see that, in addition to moving to the side, your 'inside' hand actually moves forward – and this happens without having to advance your upper arm. Although, as explained earlier (A General Note About the Aids and Communication) the *precise* way in which you apply any aid will depend to some extent upon the horse and the circumstances, as a generality, think in terms of an outward/forward movement of just a couple of inches as the 'norm' for an inside rein aid when turning. (As indicated at the start of this section, this does depend on the fact that you have a light, but distinct contact on the rein.)

Readers who have picked up the points made in the section on Rein Contact might ask: 'If my inside hand moves forward, won't I be giving away the rein contact? The first point in response to this is that, since we are talking about a small outward/forward movement, the 'outward' element will help to take up the slack that would otherwise be produced by the 'forward' element (see diagram). The second response refers back to the earlier illustration of walking in a circle by yourself. We saw that, when walking in a circle, it is natural to turn your head *slightly* in the direction of the circle – and the same applies to alignment of your other body parts. If you walk in a straight line, and then turn onto a circle, your shoulders won't stay aligned (at 90 degrees) to the original straight line. Instead, they'll tend to align naturally to a radius of the circle. The same sort of thing will happen when you ride onto a circle or through a turn on a horse. Although, as a rider, you are being carried through the turn, rather than going through it under your own steam, it will still be natural for you to look in the direction of the turn, and to turn your shoulders (slightly and naturally – not as an overt act) in the same direction. When you do this, your inside shoulder will come back slightly and your outside shoulder will move forward slightly. This will mirror and influence the movement you require from the horse, which is to adopt the line of the turn with his head and neck, and follow through with his shoulders (i.e. you don't want him to '*fall*' through the turn with his inside shoulder, or 'lean out' with his outside shoulder, as though he were trying to continue on a straight line). If the horse is to turn his head and neck in the desired fashion, this will require the muscles on the outside of his neck to stretch a little, and those on the inside to contract a little. The slight turning of your own shoulders helps to accommodate this movement: your outside shoulder and hand, moving forward slightly, allow the horse's neck to stretch without increasing the rein contact; your inside shoulder and hand, moving back slightly, 'neutralises' the effect of the 'forward and out' action of your inside elbow, and prevents the inside rein contact from being lost. (As described, these movements of hands and shoulders are somewhat arbitrary: as your 'feel' for the rein contact improves, you will find yourself making very minor, almost subconscious, alterations to them so that the contact remains as you feel it should be. An analogy would be that, whereas a learner driver/motorcyclist responds to minor deviations in the road, changes in camber and sudden gusts of wind with conscious and slight over-corrections of steering, the experienced driver maintains position on the road through the most subtle and automatic of adjustments.)

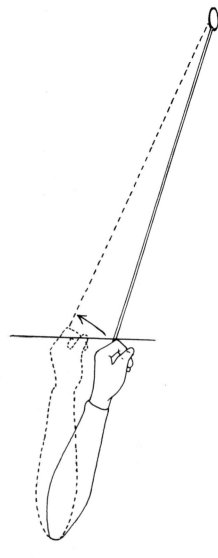

Opening the inside hand to indicate the required direction of movement. So long as the elbow is not drawn back, the movement of the hand is sideways and very slightly forward.

So, while it is important that the hands, via the reins, act subtly and accurately, what they are really doing is 'showing' the horse the way you want him to turn. It is mainly your legs that mould his body to the required shape and assist him to 'flow' smoothly round the turn. Your inside leg steady on the girth (not coming on and off) acts as a 'point of reference' for the horse – a sort of inside rail that tells him, 'You must stay to the outside of this marker.' This leg can also be used actively as necessary (firm inward pressure, not coming on and off) to encourage the horse to maintain his activity, stimulating his inside hind leg to keep stepping forward under his body and helping him to retain his balance. Your outside leg comes back a little behind the girth, resting against the horse's side and providing the outside 'channel' through which he should 'flow'. It can also act positively as required (inward pressure) to dissuade him from swinging his hindquarters to the outside. Although, as we've seen, the horse may be almost compelled to do this by incorrect use of the inside rein, he may also see it as the 'easy option' if he's not very active, well balanced or supple (flaws that are quite common in many riding school horses). In fact, 'steering' problems caused by these deficiencies may require quite strong use of the rider's legs to minimise their effects – but these effects are *never* solved by incorrect rein aids (see also Circling).

Looking naturally in the direction of the turn will produce slight changes in your shoulder alignment which will accommodate the movement you require from the horse.

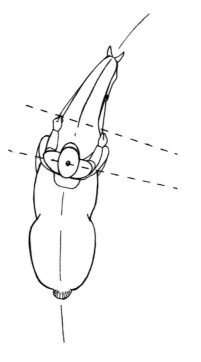

The horse should 'flow' through the channel indicated by the rider's legs.

Another aspect of the 'firm inside leg at the girth/outside leg back position' is that it tends to place additional weight in the rider's inside seat bone, which is another useful aid in getting the horse to turn because, as explained in A Word about the Seat, horses naturally tend to turn/move in the direction of the rider's weight. This 'weighted seat aid' is, in fact, a major item in the experienced rider's toolkit – advanced riders make much subtle use of these aids. However, I would stress the term 'subtle' here – you will not help a horse to turn smoothly by leaning over or throwing a lot of your weight to the inside.

PART 3

Gaits and Transitions

This section deals with aspects of learning to ride at walk, trot and canter and how to change from one gait to another.

A Word on Walk

Walk is the gait that instructors will use to introduce the first stages of riding. It is the easiest gait for a novice rider to sit on and, because it is the slowest gait, it offers more thinking time and preparation time than the other gaits. Since there is some natural movement of the horse's head in walk, it is a useful gait in which riders can practise the 'feel' of rein contact (see that section). However, despite these benefits, many riders (and many horses, too) think of walk almost in terms of sleepwalking and the horse ends up dossing along in danger of tripping over his own shadow.

Allowing a horse to walk in this way is not just wrong – it is a missed opportunity, because maintaining an active, rhythmical walk requires a constant monitoring of the horse's movement and the precise application of any aids necessary to keep the regular rhythm of the gait, and thus to practise some of the principles outlined earlier in A Stitch in Time… A rider who has learnt to feel and retain a good, active walk will find it much easier to do the same with trot and canter than a rider who just lets the horse walk sloppily.

There are other practical reasons for getting used to expecting the horse to walk out well:

1 A horse who is inactive at walk is likely to be on his forehand and thus unbalanced (see The Horse's Balance and What 'On the Forehand' Means), so it will be hard to ride accurate figures on him.

2 A combination of lack of balance and being 'switched off' (the reason for the inactivity) may, in certain circumstances, cause him to stumble – perhaps if the school is riding deep or, more crucially, on slippery or rough surfaces when riding out.

3 A horse who is 'switched off' is more likely, if startled, to react violently than one whose attention is on the job in hand. (We are the same – something is more likely to 'make you jump' if you are daydreaming than if you are really concentrating on a job at hand.)

In order to ensure that the horse is nicely active in walk, it is first necessary to monitor the rhythm of the gait. This should be a positive 1,2,3,4 as he sets each foot down in turn. If the rhythm is obviously laboured and he is patently on a 'go slow' (e.g. not keeping up with other horses of similar size), then he needs to be asked for more activity. Sometimes, if he is simply having an idle moment, a stronger leg aid backed up, if necessary, with a slap from the whip (see Uses of a Whip) will have the desired effect.

Regarding leg aids for walk, there's an important point that your instructor probably won't mention in your very early lessons but hopefully will explain at a reasonably early stage. Whereas the initial aid to go from halt to walk involves the rider using both legs equally and simultaneously, once the horse is walking, any 'refresher' leg aids should really be given rather differently. When a horse is walking, he moves both legs on one side of his body in turn, then both legs on the other side in turn – for example, left hind, left fore, right hind, right fore. As we saw earlier (Why They're Called Aids), the signals a rider sends to the horse are most effective if they are given at a time when it is easiest for the horse to respond to them. When we are asking a horse to walk on more actively, rather than applying pressure from both our legs simultaneously, it makes sense to apply pressure from each leg individually at a moment when the horse's hind legs on the same side as our leg aids are best able to respond; that is, just as he is starting to step forward with that leg. Trying to do this the first few times you sit on a horse (when your mind will be full of more pressing matters) would be rather unrealistic but, once you are a little more experienced, your instructor can help you to feel the movement of the horse's hind legs and harmonise your leg aids with them, making your aids more effective.

One indication of the hind leg movement is that, as the horse walks, his ribcage bulges slightly to one side then the other, in time with the movements of his legs. If your own legs are resting against the horse's sides, they will feel this bulging alternately and, if an active aid is necessary, it should be given at this moment. Initially, the instructor may have to say: 'Left, right, left, right' to help your timing but, pretty soon, you will develop a 'feel' for the horse's movement.

You will find that leg aids applied at the appropriate moment are vastly more effective in regulating the walk than 'on-off, on-off' aids applied in pairs – only one of which (at most) can have any logical meaning for the horse.

Having made these points about keeping the walk active, I should now present the other side of the coin. 'Active' does not mean 'rushed': if the rhythm tends towards a 1-2...3-4 count (two steps in rapid succession, a pause, then two more rapid steps) the horse is hurrying out of the correct form of the gait. This can happen if a rider just nags/drives relentlessly with the legs without due regard for how the horse is moving. This over-activity on the rider's part is often accompanied by 'shoving' with the seat (see the warning about driving seat aids in A Word about the Seat) and attempting to 'row' the horse along with the hands. While experienced riders *do* use seat aids to encourage forward movement in the horse, and their hands *do* mirror the movement in the horse's head (in order to keep the rein contact constant), these are subtle movements, unlike the arbitrary, overt movements just described.

So, while 'dossing' should not be permitted, it is also the case that a good walk cannot be achieved or maintained simply by 'getting on the horse's case', and this brings us back to the point made at the start of this section that an active walk in good rhythm requires constant monitoring and precise application of the aids *necessary* in order to maintain it.

There is a consensus amongst top trainers that the walk is the *hardest* gait to improve and the *easiest* gait to spoil. If these people think of it in this way, perhaps the rest of us should pay it more attention.

To assist activity in walk, apply the leg aids alternately when the horse can respond to them.

Rising Trot

This is the form of riding at the trot in which the rider goes up and down gently in rhythm with the beat of the gait. It was used originally in bygone days when horses were a major means of transport and riding long distances over rough ground and unmade roads was commonplace. Remaining seated in the saddle at trot in these conditions is stressful for the backs of both horse and rider (and for the latter's backside), and riders figured out that easing their seat out of the saddle on alternate beats of the trot was more comfortable for both parties.

Protracted trotting on rough or hard surfaces (e.g. trotting along the road) remains the key reason for rising to the trot – although it is also used when riding young horses who haven't developed much strength in their hindquarters and back, and other horses who have a weakness in these areas. Also, experienced riders, who have full muscular control, may sometimes use slight changes in the precise way they rise in order to influence the horse's movement and rhythm.

For these reasons, rising trot is very useful, but sometimes too great an emphasis is put on it, for the wrong reasons.

Since trot has only two beats to a stride, it is the least smooth of the horse's gaits, and it can feel distinctly bumpy to a beginner, especially one whose basic position in the saddle needs more refinement. Some instructors, therefore, put a lot of emphasis on teaching rising trot at an early stage, not so much for its real value, but more as a means of their pupils 'escaping' the bumpiness of the gait. If this is overdone it is a disservice to the pupils because it is a fact that, in order to ride to any reasonable standard, it is essential to be able to sit in the saddle and absorb the horse's movement at all gaits. (That is not to say that a rider will *always be doing this* – but it is necessary *to be able to*.) If too much emphasis, for too long, is put on the rising trot, it will become increasingly difficult for the rider to learn to sit to it. Another consequence of over-emphasising the rising trot is that this is likely to extend from the principle into the action itself, with pupils making too much effort and rising far too high.

So, what points need bearing in mind in order to produce a practical, useful, rising trot?

1 You have to start off from a reasonably correct position – in particular, your ankles need to be pretty much vertically beneath your hips. If you

start off from a markedly 'chair seat', with your legs out in front of your seat, it will be virtually impossible to rise at all, without either first leaning your upper body a long way forward (which weakens the usefulness of your seat and legs), or pulling yourself up with the reins (which is a major no-no – the horse will hate it, and will either stop or hollow his back and try to run away from the discomfort). Another point is that your stirrup leathers should be adjusted correctly to suit you – if they are too long, you will feel in danger of losing them when you start trotting; if they are too short, they may cause you to rise too high.

2 Assuming your position is all right, the next thing you need is an active, rhythmical trot. Obviously, you can't rise to the trot unless the horse is trotting. Having said this, it is a common error amongst novice riders to try to start rising the moment they feel the horse start to trot. If you do this, one of two things may happen. If the horse is a bit lazy, he might interpret the fact that you are taking your seat 'off' him as meaning that you didn't really want him to trot, and just slump back into walk. On the other hand, if, in trying to go 'with' the trot before it is established, you get a bit out of rhythm and balance (and especially if this involves hanging on to the reins), you will be making it difficult for the horse to trot freely and he will have every excuse for returning to walk. Even if he does keep trotting under these circumstances, it is very unlikely that you and he will be in harmony.

For this reason, experienced riders who wish to perform rising trot will actually sit for the first two or three strides, in order to establish the gait, before they rise to it. So, in fact, you need to be able to do at least *a little* sitting trot before you start rising.

3 Trot having two beats to each stride, the idea is that you rise on one and sit on the other. To do this, you need to listen to and 'feel' the beats and – further to the points made in 2 above, this will be much easier if the horse is active, and moving in a regular rhythm.

4 Once you can feel the rhythm, all you have to do is ease the weight from the rear of your seat on one beat, and let it return to the saddle on the next. A couple of important points here:

- The motion is essentially one of *allowing* – it is nearer to being passive rather than overtly active. To rise, you more or less *allow* the movement of the horse's back to lift you gently in the saddle; to sit, you *allow* gravity to take you back down.

- The rising motion should be a small one; the rear of your seat just leaves the saddle; the front of it remains lightly in contact.

- During the rising phase, a *very, very slight* forward inclination of your upper body will help you stay in harmony with the horse.

- The horse's head remains virtually still in trot, so your hands should do the same. This is more likely to happen in the early stages if you keep the rising motion small – it is when people rise too high and lose balance that they lose control of their hands.

As mentioned earlier, many beginners start off by rising far too high out of the saddle (a habit that can become ingrained). While this may, to some extent, be encouraged by overemphasis of the rising trot as a concept, other, more specific reasons for this are:

1 A misconception that this is 'correct' – this is simply not so.

2 A misconception that the extra effort they are making will somehow encourage the horse to trot more actively. Mechanically, there is absolutely no reason why it should do so. In practice, because the rider who rises too high is more likely to lose balance and get out of rhythm with the horse, it is more likely that the horse will become less active, rather than more so.

3 Mechanical error (whether from misconception or not); rising by standing in the stirrups, thereby straightening their legs and prising the whole of their seat out of the saddle. Doing this makes the seat ineffective and, because the legs are being employed primarily to lift the rider's body, they are less able to give any aids necessary to keep the horse going forward actively, (see the box on page 76) and to steer him. In correct rising trot, the actions of the seat should be supported by the rider's thighs, rather than the stirrups. (It is, in fact, perfectly possible to perform rising trot without stirrups, and your instructor may demonstrate this. For all but the truly riding fit, this does become tiring after a while but, for short periods, riding in this way should not com-promise the quality of the rising. Once you've had a bit of practice at rising trot, your instructor may suggest that *you* try it without stirrups,

perhaps down one long side of the school. Provided that you are able-bodied, if you can't make a reasonably good go of this, then the way you are doing your basic rising is wrong!)

One other point about rising to the trot is the question of 'diagonals'. Most instructors won't introduce this idea until pupils are established in the basics of rising trot, but will explain its relevance at the appropriate

Rising too high in trot will do nothing to assist the horse; the main effect is to disturb the rider's rhythm and balance and thereby impede the horse's movement.

If, while doing rising trot, you think that the horse is rather inactive and needs leg aids to send him on more, these aids must be given at the moment when your seat is in the saddle – it is very difficult to give these aids during the 'rising' phase and riders who try to do so usually end up putting the effort they intend to go into 'squeezing' with the legs into rising higher instead. In fact, if you think that a horse really needs urging on, it is better to remain in sitting trot (see next section) until the horse responds to your leg aids, and return to rising only when he is moving forwards actively.

time. As we've seen, the horse trots by moving his legs in diagonal pairs and, when he is trotting in an arena, where he will be turning or circling on a regular basis, it will be of some assistance to his balance if his rider 'sits' as the horse's outside shoulder comes back. In due course, you will be able to feel this, but initially it can be seen quite clearly by a brief glance down. When they have explained the concept, some instructors will conduct little exercises, asking pupils to say whether or not they are on the correct diagonal. These exercises have value in developing riders' 'feel' for what is going on beneath them. (The ability to perceive how the horse is moving underneath you is a great asset to all aspects of riding – 'feeling' the diagonal is an early introduction.)

If you wish to 'change the diagonal', all you have to do is sit for one beat of the trot, during which you would otherwise have risen, and then rise on the next beat. This should be done whenever you change direction in the school, so that your change of rising and sitting mirrors the fact that the horse has changed his 'inside' and 'outside' diagonals.

When you reach the stage of hacking out, even if you are going more or less in straight lines, you should change the diagonal on a regular basis, because if a horse is continually ridden on one diagonal only, this will contribute towards uneven muscular development and lead to him becoming 'one-sided'. (If you ride a horse whose development is going in that direction, you will notice that it is much more comfortable to rise on one diagonal than the other. Sacrificing your own comfort, and spending more time on the uncomfortable diagonal, will give you an early opportunity to involve yourself in remedial schooling.)

Sitting Trot

In many sports, there are certain skills and abilities that are really key to success – things that make a real, substantial difference to overall performance. In tennis and squash, for example, even if hitting on one side of the body comes much more naturally than the other, it is essential to become reasonably proficient on both the backhand and forehand. In golf, establishing a good technique for getting out of bunkers will help enormously – even though the ideal is to avoid them in the first place!

As mentioned in the section on rising trot, in order to ride to any reasonable standard, it is *essential* to be able to sit in the saddle and absorb the horse's movement at all gaits. This ability rarely comes naturally – in fact, many people really have to work at it – but, for anyone keen to progress, this just means that the sooner they start, the better.

Again, as mentioned earlier, trot is the 'bumpiest' of the gaits so, if you can learn to absorb the movement of trot, this will stand you in good stead for canter. Canter is, itself, smoother than trot but, in order to be able to ride good, smooth transitions from trot to canter and, especially, from canter down to trot, the ability to sit well in trot is essential. Also, if you can develop a good seat for sitting trot, that same 'adhesive', 'absorbing' seat will aid your security enormously if ever a horse you are riding bucks, spooks or shies.

The essence of developing this type of seat is to 'teach' the muscles of the seat and pelvic area to act like a big shock absorber: instead of clenching/tensing these muscles, which will add to the 'bounce factor', they must 'allow' the horse's movement into this area, and damp it down. Of course, we all learn from experience that when someone (especially a doctor or osteopath) tells us: 'Try to relax', that is code for: 'This will hurt.' However, in this case, that is essentially what you need to do and no, it won't hurt – but it might need some practice.

A useful way to introduce pupils to sitting trot (but one that is quite rarely seen), is for a helper to lead the horse in walk while the rider, sitting up straight in the saddle, grasps the pommel (front arch) of the saddle firmly with the outside hand and effectively 'pulls themselves ' down into the saddle. The helper then leads the horse into an active trot and the rider, still pulling down, practises 'letting' the horse's movement into their seat. As with practising most unfamiliar physical activities, this is best done for short periods only (which also avoids the helper collapsing with fatigue). A big advantage from the rider's point of view is that, with someone else to control the horse, they can concentrate exclusively on sitting. This, of course, also applies to learning the technique on the lunge (see Lunge Lessons). There are also broadly parallel activities that you may do out of a riding context which can give you the opportunity to practise absorbing movement. One is riding a bicycle or motorbike down uneven, bumpy roads (if you are an habitual cyclist or biker, you may have a big advantage in the sitting trot stakes); another is sitting on a bumpy commuter train, trying to read the paper. Again, if you can do this without getting double vision or bringing up your breakfast, you are a good way along the road.

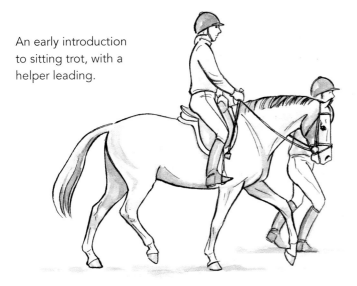

An early introduction to sitting trot, with a helper leading.

Some instructors, when developing their pupils' ability to sit to the trot, make quite a lot of use of riding without stirrups. My feeling is that, while this can be useful at an appropriate stage (and while you should certainly be able to do it in due course), it should not be done too early i.e. before pupils have displayed some ability to do sitting trot *with* stirrups. The reason for this is that, if pupils feel insecure without stirrups, they will be more inclined to tense up which, as we've seen, is the opposite of what is required. Also, this tension may involve gripping with the legs (which may send the horse into a fast 'running' trot or be misinterpreted as a signal to canter) and/or hanging on to the reins, which is always undesirable.

As I said at the start of this section, the bottom line (to make a bad pun) is that the ability to sit to the trot has benefits that go way beyond the act of trotting – so don't be tempted to avoid sitting trot, even if it feels a bit difficult at first.

Starting to Canter

Canter is the next gait up from trot. Some riders (and, it must be said, some instructors) make a big deal about starting to canter – but if riders are introduced to it at the right stage, and with correct explanations, it shouldn't be difficult.

One of the biggest misconceptions among novice riders is that a horse must trot faster *in order* to canter. This is completely untrue. In the first instance, a horse goes faster *because* he canters, not *in order to do so* (see also Transitions). In fact, a moderately well-trained horse, with a moderately competent rider, can go easily from walk directly into canter, and a more highly trained partnership will be able to take canter from halt. If you doubt this last point, consider racehorses in the starting stalls – they go into *gallop* from halt.

In a good riding school, pupils will not be asked to canter until they are reasonably secure and effective in trot. The core reasons for this are:

- When horses are cantering, they will be going *a bit* faster than pupils have gone previously, so riders first need to feel happy at an active trot, and used to steering round the arena at trot speed.

- Although a rhythmic canter is quite smooth (in fact, a good canter is generally considered the most pleasant gait for the rider), it is mechanically speaking quite a complex gait. Getting the feel of the canter and being able to go 'with' the horse's movement should come quite easily to riders *if they've had a reasonable amount of experience at trot – especially sitting trot.*

However, if a rider feels unbalanced and insecure in canter, stops riding the horse forward and hangs on to the reins, then the horse will probably 'fall' into a fast, running, trot, which will be very hard to sit on securely.

The other point related to experience at trot is that, in order to go smoothly from trot into canter, it is necessary to do a few strides of sitting trot to prepare for and apply the canter aids. Usually, instructors will start off by telling pupils to give these aids when the horse is going through a corner – the reason for this is that, so long as the horse is correctly bent through the corner (i.e. his body is curved slightly to the inside of the bend) this will help him to strike off on the correct 'leading leg'.

The 'leading leg' is an aspect of canter that doesn't apply in the same way to walk and trot. As we've seen, in walk, the horse moves both legs on one side of his body (one at a time), then both legs on the other side in the same way. In trot, he moves his legs in diagonal pairs (one hind leg and the diagonally opposite foreleg together, then the other diagonal pair). In their own different ways, both these gaits can be considered symmetrical. Canter, however, is asymmetrical; the horse moves one hind leg, then the other hind leg and the diagonally opposite foreleg together, then the final foreleg. It is this single foreleg that is known as the 'leading leg' and, if this leg is on the inside of any turn or circle, it will be easier for the horse to keep balanced. If the horse's right foreleg is leading, he is said to be 'in right canter'; if his left foreleg is leading, he is 'in left canter' (see the box on page 82). The way in which the canter aids are given will help signal to the horse which 'lead' is required.

Because, as mentioned, canter is quite a complex gait, it is also possible for the correct sequence of footfall to be disrupted in various ways other than simply being on the 'wrong leg'. When this happens, a horse is said to be cantering 'disunited'. Again, an instructor should spot this and point out the reasons for it.

The general elements of asking for a transition to canter are:

1 Rider sitting upright in active sitting trot.

2 Horse's head flexed *slightly* in the direction of required lead (inside rein *very slightly* open – not pulled back. (This flexion will happen automatically if the horse is being ridden correctly through a corner or on a circle.)

3 The rider's inside leg is at the girth (reaching well down, without the rider leaning to the inside) and:

4 Rider's outside leg moves back behind the girth (without any exaggerated bending upward of the lower leg).

With the legs in these positions, they apply pressure to ask for canter. (Ideally, the legs aids are accompanied by a forward and downward action of the inside seat bone – with advanced horse/rider partnerships this may become the most significant canter aid. However, the degree to which this is emphasised by instructors at an early stage will be dependent on the pupil's seat/balance and the

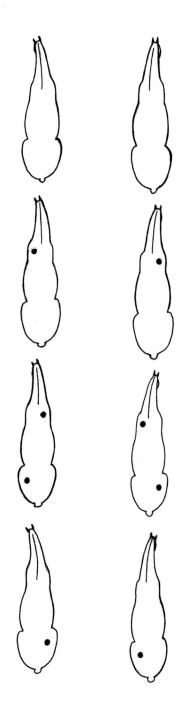

Sequence of footfall in canter; 'left lead' and 'right lead' on left and right respectively.

It *is* possible for a horse to canter with his right foreleg leading when turning left, and vice versa. With a horse in a fairly advanced stage of training, an experienced rider may do this deliberately, to improve the horse's suppleness, balance and obedience, and to prepare him for even more advanced work. This is known as counter-canter. However, when a horse does it more or less accidentally, perhaps because he has become unbalanced and/or confused by the rider's signals, he is said to be 'on the wrong leg'. To a rider who has some experience of cantering on the correct lead, this will feel generally a bit bumpy and odd. If it happens, the instructor should notice it and tell the pupil to return quietly through trot to walk, before explaining *why* it happened and suggesting another try.

instructor's own view on how to introduce the use of seat aids (see A Word About the Seat). Also see the box on page 83.

The basic roles of the rider's legs in these positions are that the outside leg stimulates the horse's outside hind leg to help initiate the change to canter and the inside leg helps with the impulsion. Once the canter is established, the rider's outside leg stays back a little and helps to prevent the horse's hindquarters from swinging outwards, especially through turns and on circles. The rider's inside leg retains its role of ensuring activity and correct bend: these functions also, are particularly important when turning and circling because they help the horse to stay in good balance.

To develop the theme of activity, it is a fact that in canter, as in the other gaits, a horse may sometimes be less active than is desired. If this inactivity is marked, the horse won't be able to maintain canter and will 'fall' into trot – or even walk. Where they see insufficient activity in canter, some instructors advise pupils to 'push' or 'drive' with the seat. (This is different from, for example, telling a rider who has 'curled up' and taken their seat 'off' the saddle to sit up straight.) Now, as mentioned earlier (A Word about the Seat) an accomplished rider, who has developed a truly deep seat and a stable position, can use the seat to influence the horse positively in various ways – including producing more activity.

I'm not trying to confuse the issue, but there's something I should point out. Because canter is quite complex, over the years different people have used different combinations of aids to achieve it. Some trainers have, in fact, used one set of aids to introduce it to young horses and then weaned them on to different aids later. Nowadays, although there is more general consensus on the canter aids, it remains the case that different instructors may place slightly more or less emphasis on different points of detail so, if you change instructors or schools, you may find that you are told to do things slightly differently, and that horses at one school may differ slightly in their response compared to those of another school. Elsewhere, I make the point that the communication side of riding is rather like learning a language, and we might say that variations of this sort are the riding equivalent of 'regional accents'.

However, when less experienced riders are advised to 'push' with the seat what often happens is a crude 'grinding' effect, accompanied by a rocking to and fro of the upper body. Far from encouraging more activity, this rocking of the rider just serves to unbalance the horse, who will also tend to 'hollow' his back away from the rider's 'grinding' action – and this, as we saw earlier (Very Basic Mechanics) will make it *harder* for him to engage his hind legs. In order to retain some semblance of balance, the horse may 'fall' out of canter into a fast, running trot – which is neither easy nor comfortable to sit on. From this situation, there is virtually no chance of salvaging the canter; the rider will have to return to walk then re-establish a good trot, before asking for a new transition to canter. Another possible outcome of rocking at canter, is that, while doing this, the rider may seek more support from the reins, and any pulling back on these will both accentuate the horse's 'hollowness' *and* act as a 'stopping' signal. In these circumstances, the horse will be more or less obliged to give up the unequal struggle to canter in the face of adversity. So, in the early stages at least, you would be better advised to keep your seat 'quiet' in canter and to use your legs in the way described earlier to keep the canter active.

Left: rider correctly upright with relatively 'quiet seat' in canter. *Right:* rider rocking back trying to drive with seat; horse in hollow outline.

Intentional downward transitions from canter (as distinct from 'losing' it) are not particularly easy to do *well*; there are some ideas that may help with them in the section on Transitions.

Cantering effectively across country, as you may do once you have started riding outdoors, requires some adaptations of posture and commonsense consideration for others in your group. We will look at these issues later under Cantering in the Open.

Transitions

Transitions are changes from one gait to another, or to and from halt. Upward transitions are from a slower to a faster gait; downward transitions from a faster to a slower one (see the box opposite). To start with, let's look at some important principles that apply to all transitions – understanding them will help you to apply the mechanics correctly:

1 You do not need to speed up or slow down *in order* to change gait – that happens *because* you change gait (see the box opposite).

2 The *quality* of the transition (its smoothness) is very closely linked to the quality of the gait that precedes it – faults such as hurrying, lack of

balance, inactivity, etc. will all be reflected in the quality of the transition. Therefore, before you ask for a transition, it is important that the horse feels active (but not hurrying), balanced and attentive.

3 In *all* transitions between gaits, you must think *forward*. Now, if you want to do an upward transition (e.g. from walk to trot), it is pretty obvious that you will think forward, because you want the horse to go forward more. However, if you want to do a downward transition, you should also think *forward* rather than *backward*. Why is this? Well, in the first place, you don't want to go backwards – you want to keep going forwards, but in a 'lower gear'. Suppose you are riding a bike, or driving your car, up a steep hill – you will probably need to change down a gear or two, but in such an instance you don't also brake or reverse. The second point relates to the horse's balance and we'll discuss this in more detail when we look at the specifics of downward transitions.

The terms 'slower and faster' are *generally* true. The gaits can be thought of as being the horse's 'gears', insofar as, when a walking horse wants to go a bit faster, he'll start to trot; if he's trotting and he wants to go a bit faster than that, he'll canter, etc. However, just as a motorised vehicle has the capacity to go at a certain speed in perhaps a choice of three gears, or at a range of speeds in the same gear, so does a horse. A well-trained dressage horse will be able to do an extended trot (very lengthened strides) which is faster in mph than his collected canter (shortened, bouncy strides). These niceties may not seem that important for novice riders, but understanding the concept, and being aware that horses can change the way they move *within* a gait, will help you to pick up on fluctuations of speed and activity that you feel in your general riding.

Upward Transitions

The basic aids for all upward transitions are very similar: having checked that the horse is active and attentive (this is the 'prepare' phase of giving aids – see Timing Aids) increased leg pressure gives a clearly defined aid and a *slight* softening of the rein contact encourages the horse to respond. (As explained in Starting to Canter, the aids for this gait are applied asymmetrically simply to help signal the required 'leading leg' – the basic principles remain the same.) The rider's intentions will be clearer to the horse if:

1 The leg aids *are* clearly defined – that is to say, if the horse hasn't previously been confused by incessantly 'chattering', 'nagging' legs that have no obvious meaning to him (see Using Your Legs). Note that, so long as the horse hasn't been 'deafened' by chattering legs, 'clearly defined' can mean just that – 'distinct', as opposed to 'big'.

2 The legs act *fractionally* before the rein contact is eased (the 'ask' and 'allow' phases of giving aids).

3 The easing of the contact *is very slight* – think of it as a subtle confirmation of what your legs are telling the horse. (If, for example, you 'throw the contact away' when asking for a transition from trot to canter, the horse may think that, instead of being asked to change gait, he is being asked to go into a fast, 'running' trot.)

Downward Transitions

We'll look at transitions to halt before discussing other downward transitions, because there are lessons to be learnt from halting that are useful when riding downward transitions in general.

In the early stages, you will only be expected to halt from walk and, since you will need to stop to get off the horse, your first experience of halting will come very early on. The key point that your instructor will (or should) make is that, contrary to popular opinion and to the evidence of every Western you've ever seen, halting need not and certainly should not involve pulling back on the reins. An exercise that some instructors use to demonstrate this is to ask a pupil to walk the horse on a long rein, with minimal rein contact, then get the pupil to imagine very strongly that, at a certain point in the school, they themselves are going to 'splat' very hard into a concrete wall, as though they were hitting it at speed. The pupil is not to make any conscious effort to alter the rein contact.

When a rider does this with conviction, the horse (even if he does

Upward transitions:
(*top*) halt to walk;
(*centre*) walk to trot;
(*bottom*) trot to canter.

not perform a perfectly square, balanced halt) will invariably stop. Why does this happen? Well, it isn't any spooky telepathic communication. When the rider imagines a full-on splatting, they will stop using any 'forward-urging' leg aids, subconsciously brace their back (see A Word About the Seat) and put some more weight into their seat – producing a 'holding' effect, which the horse (who is being sat upon, and is sensitive to such things) will pick up. Also, although the rider hasn't done anything consciously to the reins, the bracing of the back will have *slightly* increased the tension in them.

Now, although this exercise makes some important points, I'm not suggesting that it is the usual or correct way to ask for 'proper' halts. Prior to halting, you will normally want the horse to be walking actively, with your reins at a length that permits a light but definite contact. To obtain the halt:

- Think of sitting up a little more and 'stopping' the movement of your upper body (this will produce the holding effect as described in the 'splatting' exercise).

- Stop giving the alternate 'forward' aids with your legs (see A Word on Walk), but keep them resting against the horse's sides.

- Quietly 'stop' your hands from following the movement of the horse's head (see A Word on Walk).

The idea is that the horse halts in response to stepping forward into your still hands.

If the halt is to be maintained for any length of time, it is useful to relax these aids *just a fraction* to let the horse know that he has done what you required.

Moving on to other downward transitions, it is a fact that they are harder to ride well than upward transitions, the fundamental reason for this being that they are harder for the horse to do. Riding them well requires practice, the development of 'feel' and the watchful eye and input of a good instructor. That said, understanding what you are trying to achieve can only help the learning process.

We have seen (Very Basic Mechanics) that the horse is 'rear-engined' and, in addition to using his back end for propulsion, it is also important that he can always bring his hind legs forward under him to remain in good balance. Now, when we ask a horse for a downward transition, it is clearly desirable that he remains in good balance and – since we want him to keep going forward actively in the new gait – it is important that he can use his hind legs to provide the propulsion. So, in a downward transition, while we need to signal to the horse that he is to 'change down a gear', we also need to encourage him to move his hind legs forward under him. This is why, earlier in this section, I made the point that, even in downward transitions, it is important to think 'forward'.

When you want to ride a downward transition from one gait to another, think about the following:

- *Imagine* that *you* want to slow down. Don't lean back, but keep very upright and think about keeping your upper body still. As explained earlier, this will produce a bracing of your lower back and a holding effect of your seat, which the horse will pick up on.

- Although you shouldn't use your legs to give the sort of 'forward' aids you would use to signal an *upward* transition, keep them resting against his sides. The idea is that they should still be 'saying' just enough to him to encourage him to keep stepping under with his hind legs, so that he can do the downward transition in balance. (This is quite a subtle process: car drivers might compare it to balancing a car on a hill with the clutch.)

- In the same way that you have thought about 'stillness' in your upper body, think about your hands becoming very still. To make another analogy, a tennis or squash player might think in terms of a stop volley where, although the racquet head is stopped, it is stopped out of a forward impulse, rather than being snatched back. A cricketer might compare the action to a defensive stroke with a 'dead bat'. If you have been working on your rein contact (see that section) you will have been developing what is sometimes called an 'elastic' contact. This does not mean that your hands will make big, obvious movements in response to movements of the horse's head, but it does mean that they will be sensitive to his movements and he, in turn, will be sensitive to your hands. Therefore, if your hands 'stop' any forward yielding, the horse will pick up on this.

As soon as the horse responds by changing down a gait, ease your 'holding' seat aid slightly, 'allow' him forward into the new gait with your hands and encourage him forward into it as necessary with your legs.

You will notice that the points made in respect of downward transitions between gaits have a lot in common with the transition into halt, but there is one major difference. Whereas halting entails the horse stopping, in other downward transitions you want him to keep moving – in a lower gait, certainly, but with a proportionate amount of activity. By this, I mean that, if a horse goes from an active trot into walk, although he will be going slower because of the change of gait, the walk should have the same degree of 'purpose' to it as the trot had. However, in the trot to walk transition in particular, a lot of horses use the transition as an excuse to 'die' on the rider and – if they are particularly lazy and the transition is (literally) heavy-handed – they may even try to stop. If the aids are given in a way that *encourages* this response, more practice is needed in co-ordinating them but, if the horse is just 'trying it on', you need to be alert to this and ready to send the horse on with your legs *the moment* you feel him change from trot to walk. This *doesn't* mean giving the horse a great kick as soon as he starts walking; it *does* mean being attuned to what is going on beneath you and correcting the horse while idleness is still just a thought in his head (see A Stitch in Time).

As mentioned in the section Starting to Canter, the downward transition from canter to trot is not easy to do smoothly, so that the horse 'flows' seamlessly into the new gait. The most fundamental reason for this is that the horse, travelling with a fair bit of momentum in canter, has to pretty much 'rebalance' himself (and rearrange his footfall) into trot. If he can't achieve this, he will either 'fall' forward into a running trot or else raise his head and neck, 'hollow' his outline and do a sort of 'emergency stop', which again won't make for a smooth transition. (See also The Horse's Balance and What 'On the Forehand' Means.)

You will see from this that any mistake the rider makes in the timing or application of the aids will be unhelpful, and getting things consistently right is likely to take some practice. Most instructors have tips to help with this, but two that will be useful in the early stages are:

1 Give the horse time. Don't ask for an abrupt transition at the last moment; start asking several strides before you need the horse to trot. (This is especially important if you are cantering to the rear of a ride – it lessens the chance that you might mistime things and crash into another horse.)

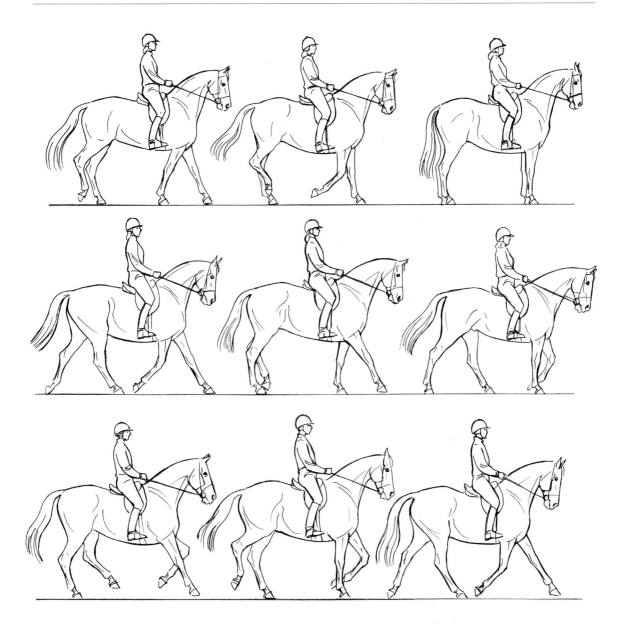

Downward transitions:
(*top*) walk to halt;
(*centre*) trot to walk;
(*bottom*) canter to trot.

2 The instructor may suggest asking for the transition on a circle because, in order to remain in canter on a circle, the horse will have to be in reasonably good balance – perhaps better than he might be if cantering in rather 'lollopy' fashion on a straight line. (It may help further if the transition is requested as the horse is heading towards the school wall – e.g. the E or B marker. This is not to suggest that he is likely to crash into the wall if he doesn't make the transition! However, his instincts at this point will be to back off slightly and steady himself, which would not apply if he was just coming out of a corner of the school onto a long side.)

The transitions mentioned in this section are called 'progressive'; that is to say, they are from one gait to the next in sequence – for example, if you want to go from halt to canter you ride into walk, then trot, then canter. At a later stage, you will start to be introduced to 'direct' transitions, in which you 'miss a gear', as in halt to trot. In fact this example will certainly be the first one you try: it is the easiest to do and it is a useful exercise in teaching a rider to retain the horse's attention at halt and then give effective leg aids. From what you have read in this section you will appreciate that direct downward transitions (e.g. canter to walk) require a good level of subtlety and co-ordination and they should be attempted only once riders are pretty accomplished.

The Horse's Balance and What 'On the Forehand' Means

I'm addressing this subject in this section on Gaits and Transitions because the horse's balance affects how he moves in all the gaits, and how well he can change from one gait to another.

In the earlier section, Very Basic Mechanics, I made a passing reference to how the horse's head and neck can affect his balance. At this point, it's worth looking a bit more at balance because, in mechanical terms, once you are sitting on a horse, you are inevitably part of the overall horse/rider unit. You can do things that assist the balance of this unit, and you can do things that destabilise it, but the only way you can disassociate yourself from it is by getting off. As ever, understanding a little more about what is involved will help you to make a positive contribution to this balance.

The horse's head and neck are often described as his balancing pole. An extreme example of how they can be used in this way occurs when a horse at liberty is careering around a field and realises that he's about to gallop into a fence. At this point, he will throw his head and neck upward (which shifts weight rapidly backwards) 'sit down' behind and brace his forelegs out in front of him. If you look around muddy fields, you will sometimes see the resultant deep furrows and skid marks just short of the fence line. 'Aha!', you say, 'contrary to what has been written earlier (Very Basic Mechanics, Posture, not Posing and Rein Contact), here is evidence that a raised head and neck are not always a bad thing.' Well, in an emergency, they may help the horse to stop suddenly, just as stamping on the clutch and brake pedals will produce an emergency stop in your car. However, an emergency stop in a car carries various risks (skids, etc.) and causes a good deal of brake and tyre wear, which is why you don't stop like this every time you come to a junction or red lights. Similarly, the horse's emergency stop can cause skidding and will place considerable strain on joints, muscles, tendons and ligaments, which is why the horse doesn't stop like that when he's trotting over to see his mates – and why you shouldn't attempt to stop like this when you're coming up behind another horse in the riding school. See the box on page 94.

An 'emergency stop' in a field. There is a big difference between what can be achieved in a desperate situation, and what is good practice in most circumstances.

Of course, the horse isn't just able to *raise* his head and neck; he can also lower them. When he does so, the basic effect is to place more weight towards his front end. When a horse lowers his head to graze, he makes

Anyone who has ever seen a display of Western-style riding may have in mind the 'sliding stop', in which the horse, travelling quickly, is brought rapidly to a spectacular halt, with a relatively raised front end and lowered back end. However, the essence of this movement lies not in the raising of the head and neck, but in the extreme lowering of the hindquarters; a theme that has associations with classical high school riding. Furthermore, this is not achieved by hauling on the reins – indeed skilled Western riders, on well-trained horses, can signal this stop through their seat alone.

adjustments to counteract this change of balance, changing the posture of his forelegs and bracing them slightly, so that (unlike some people I've known) he doesn't fall face first into his dinner. Before moving off, he will raise his head to some extent to rebalance himself.

If a ridden horse is moving with significantly lowered head and neck he will, to some extent, be unbalanced forward unless he counteracts this by rounding his back (which, as we saw in Very Basic Mechanics, includes the outline of his neck) and really using his hind limbs to step under and carry himself. If these counteractions don't happen – if his neck/back is in a 'flat' outline and his hind limbs aren't supporting him enough, he *will* be tipped forward, with additional weight on his shoulders and forelimbs. In this position, he will be more or less 'running' along to keep his balance, like a person going down a steep, slippery path and because of this, he will 'lean' on the bit in his mouth and feel heavy in the rider's hands. This sort of movement is known as 'being on the forehand' (because that's where the majority of the horse's weight is) and, in fact, the description 'downhill' is often used, because that's the sensation the rider will get.

As mentioned in the Glossary entry '**on the forehand**', some horses tend to move in this way because of their conformation. However, even in these horses, this tendency can be minimised or exacerbated by effective or ineffective riding. In the vast majority of cases, a horse going on the forehand is doing so because the rider is causing or allowing it to happen. Two examples of this are:

1 If a rider leans back in the saddle and/or hangs on to the reins (see the chair seat, in Posture, not Posing), even though more weight of the horse/rider unit will be further back, it will be physically difficult and uncomfortable for the horse to use his back end properly (see Very Basic Mechanics of the Horse) and, insofar as he is willing to go forwards at all, he will be obliged to make extra use of his front end to 'drag' himself along.

2 Even if there is no major flaw in the rider's posture, if the horse is not encouraged to step forward with his hind legs in active fashion, he may not make sufficient use of his back end to balance and carry himself and the rider and he will, again, lean forward and 'drag' himself along lazily with his front end. (Remember going back to school on the first day after the summer holiday? That's the feeling the horse will give the rider.)

Signs (from the saddle) of a horse being on the forehand are:

• Short, scuttling, steps.

• The impression that he is 'going downhill'.

• A feeling that he is 'leaning on your hands' (a dead, heavy rein contact: one of the signs most easily picked up by attention to what you can feel in your hands – see Rein Contact).

A horse going 'on the forehand' as a result of inactivity: his lazy hind limbs are doing little to propel or 'carry' him; he is 'dragging himself along' with extra weight on his front end and 'leaning' on the rider's hands.

If your instructor notices that your horse is going on the forehand, he or she will suggest an appropriate correction, depending on circumstances, but it is certain to include either a correction to your posture and/or an instruction to ask your horse for more active use of his back end (see also Half-halts).

Half-halts

Half-halts are included in this section because, used correctly, they are a great tool for improving a horse's balance – for example, correcting a tendency to go onto the forehand. They can also be used to increase the horse's attentiveness and this, combined with their balancing function, makes them helpful in preparing for changes of direction, new movements and transitions. Applied astutely they are, in fact, *very* helpful in retaining the horse's balance in the more demanding downward transitions and accomplished riders will use them routinely for such purposes.

However, like seat aids (which are components of half-halts), they need to be introduced to riders prudently and at the right stage of their skill development. If they are introduced too early and out of context, pupils may get the idea that they entail playing some kind of 'stop-go' trick on the horse, so I should emphasise that the half-halt *does not* consist of slowing the horse down until he is about to 'fall out' of his existing gait, then kicking him in the ribs.

So, what is the 'right stage' for learning about them – and what are they?

Regarding the 'right stage', riders are not in a position to give constructive half-halts until they can ride the horse forward into a consistent rein contact and are attuned to the horse's movement through the feeling they have in their hands and the activity beneath the saddle (see Rein Contact and A Stitch in Time...).

Regarding the nature of half-halts, their main 'mechanical' effect is to get the horse to take a little more weight on his back end and a little less on his front end, and they work along these lines:

1 The 'tuned-in' rider senses a need to improve the horse's balance. (This may be because the horse has got rather heavy in the hands and the rider realises he's a bit on the forehand, or simply in preparation for a turn or transition.)

2 The rider responds by sitting rather more upright, closing the shoulder blades and pushing the lower back forward a little to produce a slight bracing of the back (see A Word About the Seat) and increases leg pressure, demanding more activity.

3 The horse goes to respond to these aids, stepping more forward underneath himself.

4 However, rather than softening the rein contact slightly to allow this extra activity to produce more forward movement, the rider's hands remain still. The seat and legs are, therefore, 'pushing' the horse's back end into a gently restraining contact, in effect, 'compressing' him slightly.

5 The desired result of this is that the horse's back end lowers fractionally and his front end consequently rises a little; the horse is rebalancing himself by taking a little more weight on his back end and 'lightening' his forehand.

6 *The moment* the rider feels this improvement in balance, the half-halt aids are eased, reverting to their state before the half-halt was applied. (If the half-halt was given in preparation for a turn or transition, the aids to produce this should be given while the horse's attention and balance are in their heightened state, but they should not be hurried or clumsy. They should be saying: 'Now I've got your attention, please turn left/canter/whatever', not 'Oh heck, please turn left/canter/whatever quickly, before I lose control.')

The half-halt is a combination of seat, leg and rein aids used to improve the horse's balance and also to heighten his attention to the rider.

Properly applied, a half-halt is a subtle and momentary action (people sometimes say it should take place 'within a stride'); it is not a big action that has a long-lasting effect. If a half-halt doesn't have the desired effect, it is usually better to ease off and re-apply it, rather than keeping all the aids 'clamped on', which can seem contradictory and confusing to the horse. In order to retain good balance (or, sometimes, attentiveness) in the horse, it may be necessary to apply half-halts quite frequently – this is fine if they are given thoughtfully, for specific reasons and do not degenerate into more or less continual 'niggling'.

PART 4

Basic Figures

This section explains the value of riding certain figures and gives some tips on helping to ride them accurately.

Geography and Geometry

When you first start riding you should be in an enclosed area. This will usually be an indoor or outdoor school of set dimensions – most commonly 40 x 20 m, which is the standard size of a small dressage arena. Around the perimeter of the school will be a series of marker letters; these are standard letters which are used in dressage tests to direct the rider through the required movements. In order to fulfil this role they are (or should be) positioned at set distances from each other (see diagram overleaf).

During your first few lessons, you will be concentrating on the real basics, so the layout of the school will be of little interest to you. In time, however, it will become significant for two reasons:

1 As you learn the basic controls, your instructor will be able to direct you by reference to the arena letters, thus giving you specific points at which to do certain things ('At C trot, at M turn diagonally across the school to K').

2 The actual size and proportions of the school will influence where and how you do things.

Marker letters and layout of a 40 x 20 m arena.

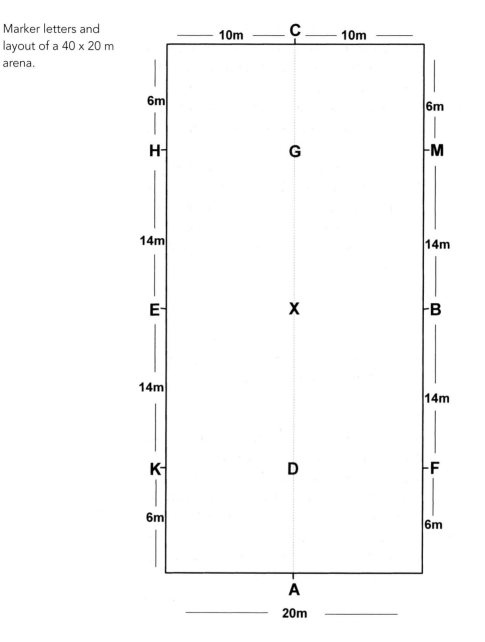

We can make an analogy here with someone learning to drive. When they are just beginning to learn about the controls, a big, empty car park can be a useful place to start. In such a place, it doesn't matter if the steering is a bit wonky, or control of the clutch and accelerator aren't very smooth. However, once they have sorted out these basics, in order to progress further they will have to start concentrating on greater precision. Turning right into the side road, rather than into a lamppost becomes an important issue, as does stopping behind, rather than in the back of, the dustcart. It's the same with riding: at some point, when you've progressed to hacking out, halting at the junction, rather than halfway out in the main road will become important, as will turning the horse through a gateway in a way that avoids a collision between your knee and a concrete post. And the way to practise these things is to learn to halt or turn accurately at the school markers.

To continue the driving analogy, if your driving instructor tells you to 'take the next right' it helps if you know roughly where the next right is, so that you can check your mirror, slow down at the right time, and manoeuvre to the appropriate spot. The same basics apply if your riding instructor tells you to 'turn across the school from E to B': if you know where these markers are, you can:

(a) prepare for the turn;

(b) know the angle at which you need to turn;

(c) give your aids in good time, so that your horse isn't suddenly hoicked around in a way that will unbalance him and cause him to lose his rhythm.

So, in due course, it will help you, your horse, your instructor and, possibly, your fellow pupils, if you can commit the relative positions of the marker letters to memory. In practice, you will probably start to absorb this information as your instructor introduces you to them in the normal course of events: 'Walk on round the school and at E – that's the marker halfway down the next long side...', 'Turn up the centre of the school from A to C...' Another way to help you learn them is to use a mnemonic – a verse or saying that helps you to repeat a series of points in order. The traditional one for remembering the sequence of markers around a 40 x 20 m arena (see the box on page 102) is:

All **K**ing **E**dward's **H**orses **C**an **M**anage **B**ig **F**ences – A, K, E, H, C, M, B, F.

You may be able to make up one of your own based on the same sequence – in all probability, the ruder it is, the more memorable it will be.

One important point to note about the markers K, H, M and F – which are called 'quarter markers' – is their positioning. These markers are *not* in the corners of the school; they are each positioned 6 m away from the corners, up the long sides of the school. This is really significant, as explained in the bullet point 'Long diagonals', in the next section, School Figures.

If you go to a school with a large (60 x 20 m) arena, you will be confronted by four extra marker letters around the perimeter. These are situated one each halfway between the quarter markers and the centre markers on the long sides (see diagram). Note that the quarter markers are still 6 m from the actual corners of the arena.

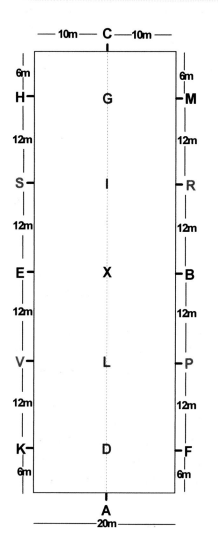

Marker letters and layout of a 60 x 20 m arena.

School Figures

Carrying on from talking about the layout of the school, it would be useful to give a brief explanation of some of the basic figures.

Riding prescribed figures in the school is a major part of training for both horses and riders. So far as horses are concerned, accurately performed figures and exercises have a significant gymnastic value and contribute to developing the horse's suppleness, balance and strength. For the rider, they develop precise control and harmony with the horse – they are not just about getting from A to B *somehow*, but getting there smoothly, accurately and with minimum effort.

School figures can increase in complexity as riders progress, and they do not necessarily have to be based on specific markers. However, at an early stage the instructor will stick to simple, basic figures and, in the interests of giving pupils definite reference points, figures will usually be described in terms of relevant marker letters.

Some basic lines and figures are as follows.

- **The long sides and short sides** are self-evident descriptions of the perimeter of the school.

- **The centre line** is the (usually imaginary) line AC (not EB). Where AC and EB intersect is the geometrical centre of the school, which is referred to as X. Although imaginary, X is used a good deal as a reference point, because of its central position.

- **The three-quarter lines** are either side of, and parallel to, the centre line, each being halfway between the centre line and the long sides of the school. These lines generally aren't used a great deal in the early stages of instruction (although see description of shallow loop on pages 108–9), but riding straight up these imaginary lines, with no walls or reference points for guidance, is a good exercise in trying to keep the horse going straight.

- **An incline** is any straight line ridden at a mild angle, from or to the outside track. For example, if you are going round the school on the left rein (anticlockwise), then turn up the centre from A and, after a stride or two, head straight for H, you are 'inclining' to the outside track.

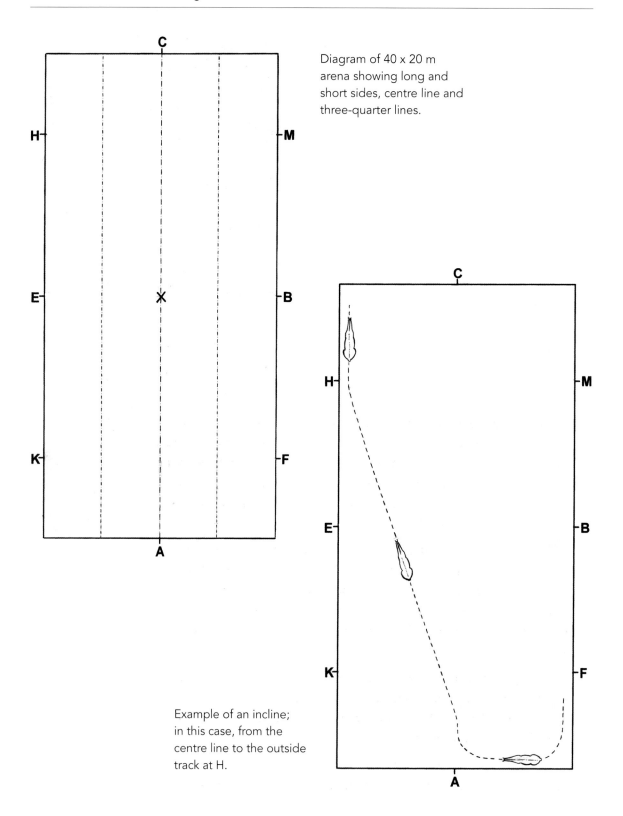

Diagram of 40 x 20 m
arena showing long and
short sides, centre line and
three-quarter lines.

Example of an incline;
in this case, from the
centre line to the outside
track at H.

- **Long diagonals** are the lines from quarter marker to quarter marker, i.e. HF (or FH) and MK (or KM), often used as a means of changing direction. For example, if you are going round the school on the right rein (clockwise) and turn onto the long diagonal KM, you will need to change direction onto the left rein when you reach the track at M.

  When riding long diagonals it is really important that you ride accurately from one quarter marker to the other, and don't go from corner to corner, which would involve two sharp turns of a type that horses aren't designed for. If you ride from quarter marker to quarter marker, this means that, after you have started down the first long side, you have a stride or two in which the horse can be straight, before he moves, at the quarter marker, onto the diagonal at quite a mild angle (an incline). Similarly, if you ride the diagonal accurately to the other quarter marker, it is fairly easy to straighten up on the outside track before going through the second corner. However, if you lose your line and head directly into the second corner, your horse won't be able to get through it without losing balance and activity.

Some of the descriptions above include practical reasons why it is helpful to always try to ride straight lines as straight as you can – doing so is also an exercise in being proactive; the more alert you are, the more readily you can correct any minor deviation and the less likely you are to end up stuck in a corner. Another point to bear in mind is that a horse going straight is almost always an active, attentive horse.

- **Circles,** in the horse world are always described in terms of their diameter, and are always measured in metres. Their location in the school is given with reference to their starting point which (with them being circular) is also their finishing point. So, for example, a 20 m circle from E starts and finishes at E and has B (opposite E at the other end of its diameter) as the halfway point.

- **A half-circle** is a half of a full circle of the same diameter so, for example, a 20 m half-circle (which some people would call 'half a 20 m circle') from E would start at E and finish at B; a 10 m half-circle from E would start at E and finish at X.

- **A serpentine** is a series of half-circles or arcs (commonly described as 'loops') of equal size, curving in alternate directions. Serpentines are

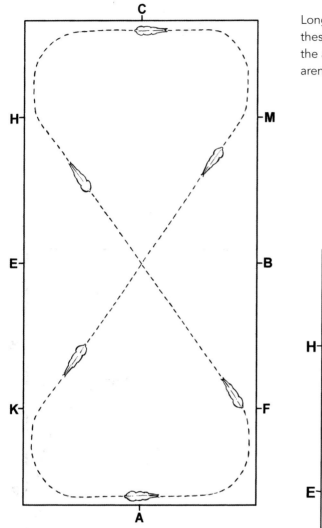

Long diagonals – note that these *don't* start or finish in the actual corners of the arena.

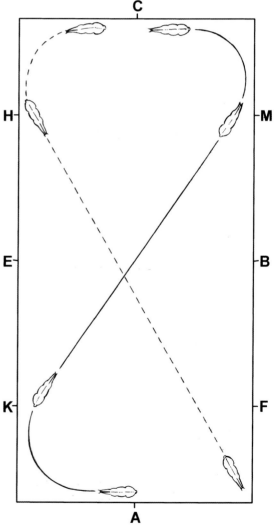

Correctly and incorrectly ridden long diagonals: the diagonal KM has been ridden correctly; the line starting from H has gone off course and, instead of reaching the track at F, the horse has gone into the corner, from where it will be impossible to turn onto the short side without loss of balance and activity.

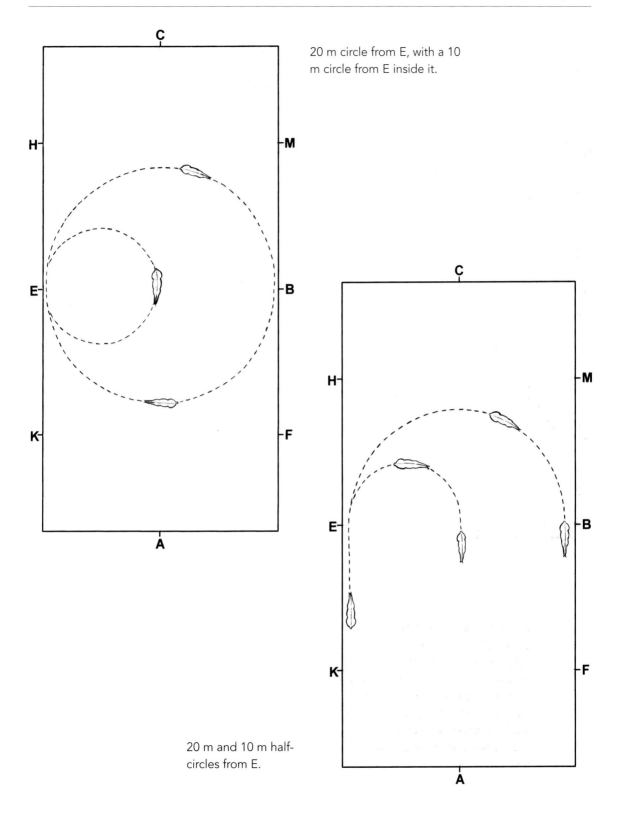

20 m circle from E, with a 10 m circle from E inside it.

20 m and 10 m half-circles from E.

usually described in terms of the total number of loops and (unless there is an instruction to the contrary), the assumption is that the overall figure will fill the school. Riding serpentines is good for practising accuracy and co-ordination of the aids.

- **A shallow loop** is essentially an arc of a very large circle (much bigger than would fit the school) ridden counter to the general direction of travel. If, for instance, you are going round the school on the left rein

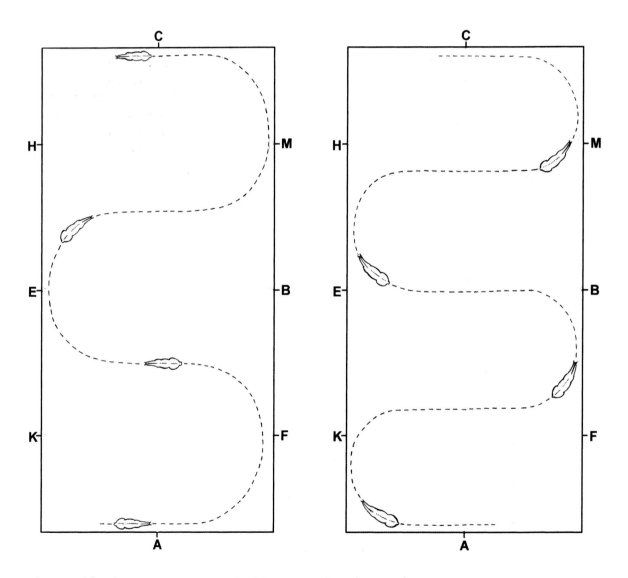

Three- and four-loop serpentines in a 40 x 20 m arena. These figures take some experience to ride well, but they are very good practice.

(anticlockwise) and are asked to ride a shallow loop between F and M, this involves coming off the outside track to the inside at F, establishing a slight bend to the right and maintaining this slight bend until you rejoin the outside track at M, at which point the horse is straightened (see diagram). The description 'shallow' usually means that, at its midpoint (level with the B marker) the loop will be about 5 m in from the track (touching the three-quarter line); occasionally a different distance may be specified, but the principle remains the same.

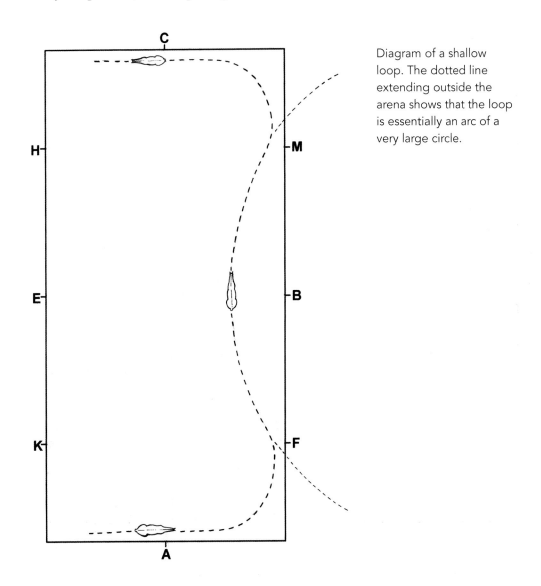

Diagram of a shallow loop. The dotted line extending outside the arena shows that the loop is essentially an arc of a very large circle.

Circling

Circles are used a good deal in riding. From the point of view of training horses, correct circle work helps improve their suppleness, balance, and the way they engage their hind legs (and thus use them actively). For riders, work on circles helps encourage proactive thinking and correct use of the aids.

Riding circles (at any rate, accurate ones in an active rhythm), is by no means easy – and both horse and rider may contribute to the difficulty for the following reasons:

- Moving on a continuous curve is mechanically harder for the horse than moving on a straight line.

- Like people, hardly any horses are truly ambidextrous; most find it relatively easy to bend in one direction, and relatively difficult to bend in the other. On this basis, you would be correct in thinking that it can be quite difficult to ride a circle in the direction to which the horse finds it difficult to bend – but it can also be quite difficult to do so in the opposite direction, because the horse may find it *too easy* to bend that way, with the result that he tends to drop in and make the circle smaller than intended. (One point arising from this is that it can be interesting to assess whether particular difficulties are consistently more apparent when circling in one direction or the other. This is the sort of thing that can help a thoughtful rider to learn more about an individual horse in particular, and the overall processes of riding in general.)

- In order to ride an accurate circle, it is first necessary to visualise it, and some people find this quite hard.

There are some simple steps an instructor can take to reduce these difficulties:

1 Keeping the circles big. The bigger the circles, the easier they are for the horse (and thus, in terms of actual riding technique, the rider). The biggest circle that can be ridden in a standard (dressage arena sized) school is 20 m diameter. As skill and accuracy increase, the circles can be made smaller.

2 Using reference points. Using the existing school markers, the easiest place to ride a 20 m circle is starting from E or B (halfway down a long side), because these two markers provide obvious visual references – the first is the starting point; the second is where the first half of the circle finishes; the second half-circle takes you back to where you started. If your instructor takes pity on you, additional markers (usually traffic cones or jump blocks) can be placed on the centre line, about 9 m either side of X. Passing just to the outside of these markers will keep your circle the right size and shape.

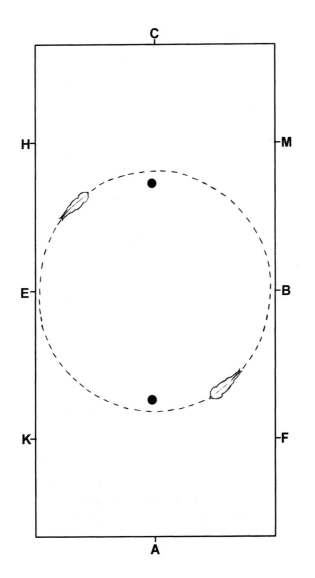

A 20 m circle ridden from E or B; this can be made easier for inexperienced riders if the instructor places markers at appropriate points on the centre line.

Quite often, instructors will ask pupils to ride a 20 m circle starting at either the A or C marker (halfway along a short side). These circles are actually very difficult for novice riders, because there are no permanent markers to show where the circle should touch the long sides of the school, and because both riders and horses are (or should be) used to going into the corners between the short and long sides – and doing this means that the figure ridden will NOT be a circle. Again, these circles can be made easier by placing markers to the inside of the long sides, 4 m past the quarter markers (which riders pass to the *outside*, and at appropriate points in the corners (which riders pass to the *inside*).

Riding a 20 m circle from the midpoint on a short side – a difficult figure to ride accurately. The instructor may use markers to give definition and dissuade pupils from going too deep into the corners.

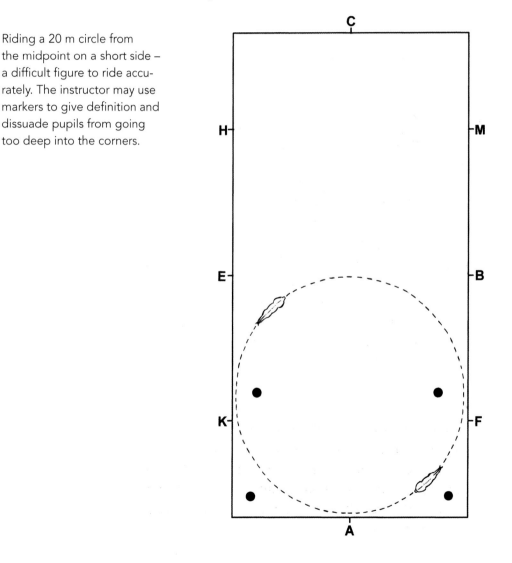

While using extra markers will help pupils to ride circles in the early stages, some people get over-reliant on them and lose their accuracy when they are removed. Such riders need to learn to visualise the figures for themselves (for instance, imagining them marked out in white paint on the school surface). One way in which instructors may 'wean them off' additional markers is to have a circle marked out at one end of the school but not the other, and have riders alternate between them.

Tips for riding circles

- **Prepare.** Before you begin the circle, make sure that the horse is going forward actively and rhythmically. If he's inactive before he starts, he's highly unlikely to increase his activity on a circle. (Although it's not desirable for a horse to be *rushing*, if he's doing so a bit before he starts the circle, his rhythm may improve on the circle, since circling can steady horses who are hurrying – but only if they're ridden very accurately.)

- **Visualise it.** If you don't have a mental picture of where you're going to go, you won't get there. This applies to how the human brain and body combine: if you are throwing a dart, or a ball, kicking a ball, hitting it with a bat or racquet, it won't go where you want it to unless you've got a picture in your mind of *where* you want it to go. The same sort of thing applies to driving: although you have to turn the steering wheel a set amount to get a set response, you do this subconsciously as a result of what your eyes are telling your brain. 'Seeing' a white line on the ground (as just mentioned) or perhaps imagining you and your horse going along a circular railway track, may be helpful. (Note this 'seeing' should be primarily a mental image – don't actually look down, because your lowered head will compromise your upper body posture.)

- **Start right.** The start of the circle and the first quarter are the key. If you don't start at the right place, you *may* still ride a circle, but it won't be the circle you wanted. That said, it is usually better to begin a circle a little further up the school than intended, and ride a good figure, than to try to haul the horse belatedly from the intended starting point onto the figure – in which case he'll start off unbalanced and probably produce a really bad imitation of a circle.

Start the circle by 'showing' the horse the way subtly with the reins (see Showing, Not Steering) and 'channel' his body onto the figure with your inside leg on the girth and your outside leg a little further back. Especially if you are trotting on an active horse, be careful to slide your outside leg quietly into position, and don't 'clamp' your legs against him, or he may interpret this as a signal to canter.

If you get the first quarter of the circle right, so that the horse is in good balance on the correct line, 'all' you have to do is keep on that line and you'll get back to your starting point. Yes, this is easier said than done, but it gives you a sporting chance! If you don't get the first quarter right, you'll spend the rest of your time 'looking' for the circle, and the chances are you won't find it.

Here is a point of encouragement about the first quarter of a circle – it is usual to ride a turn through 90 degrees (e.g. through a corner of the school, or across from one long side to the other) as a quarter of a circle. This turn will usually be a quarter of a circle that, if it were a full circle, would be a fair bit smaller than the full circles you will be asked to ride at an early stage. So, if you can ride a 90 degree turn reasonably accurately, you should be able to manage the first quarter of a larger circle.

However, in spite of your efforts to 'get the first quarter right and keep going', there are two basic problems the horse may throw at you on your journey round the circle: trying to cut in or hanging to the outside. (Although these directional wobbles can be caused by rider error, I'm assuming here that they are of the horse's making. See the box on page 116.)

If the horse is cutting in (trying to make the circle smaller), you may to tempted to try to hold him out on the circle by pulling on the outside rein. However, while this may persuade him to take a slightly wider course, there is *no possibility* that it will put him back on a correct circle. Either, he will continue with most of his body slanted inward but his head and neck turned outward (an unbalanced position that will interfere with his rhythm and forward movement), or he will swing his hindquarters to the inside of the circle and his head to the outside. What is needed instead, as soon as you sense him trying to cut in, is more positive use of your inside leg, which must say to him, 'This leg is the circumference of the circle – you shall not pass.' This is not easy for inexperienced riders to

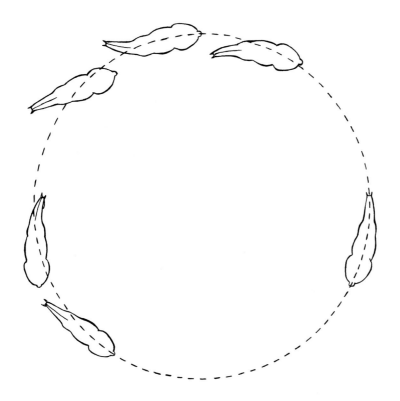

Difficulties with correct bend on a circle. *Top three images:* horse (*right*) tries to cut in on the circle: if the rider reacts simply by pulling on the outside rein, either the horse will simply bend his head and neck to the outside (*centre*) or he will turn his head and neck out and his hindquarters in, so he is aligned at an angle to the circle. *Bottom left images:* the horse who finds it difficult to bend in a particular direction (in this case, to the right) will tend to hang out on the circle. If the rider just pulls on the inside rein, this horse may be persuaded to move his head to the inside, but it's a virtual certainty that his hindquarters will swing to the outside. *Lower right:* correct alignment ('bend') on a circle.

do, but practising the two lateral exercises mentioned in the next section (especially the exercise of leg-yielding out on a corner) often improves both competence and confidence in the use of leg aids. In this case, rather than the inside leg actively 'pushing' the horse to the outside, it *resists* his attempts to lean to the inside. Furthermore, its pressure also produces more activity from the horse, which improves his balance and reduces his tendency to lean in. As I've said, this is not a particularly easy thing for a novice to put into practice, but achieving it will provide one of those

A horse may cut in as a response to a rider pulling him round on the inside rein, or hang out because the rider is hanging on to the outside rein (possibly in a crude attempt to slow him down). These faults are almost the 'opposites' of the faulty solutions mentioned in trying to correct problems of the *horse's* making.

'Eureka – I've cracked it' moments, adding considerably to your repertoire of riding skills.

The opposite problem – the horse hanging to the outside – is not caused by him trying to make the circle bigger because he wants to do more work. Most likely, it is because he is being asked to circle in the direction he finds more difficult (i.e. it is harder for him to bend his body that way). If this is a big problem with a particular horse (perhaps as a result of a past injury), the instructor should tell you this, and it is not a problem that can be fully resolved quickly or easily. However, just trying to pull the horse round on the inside rein is likely (because he has a genuine problem) to create more resistance and, if his *head* comes to the inside it is pretty well certain that his back end will swing to the outside – in this situation, what you have is a horse who just changes his orientation to the circle as you pull on the rein. As I've said, if this is an ingrained problem it really needs solving over time through remedial schooling by an experienced rider but, in the short term, you can make a contribution. Keep a firm pressure with your inside leg on the girth, and keep your outside leg back and on the horse's side. (As stated earlier, don't suddenly 'clamp' these aids on, or the horse might think you want him to canter.) With these aids you are trying to 'mould' the shape of the horse's body to conform to the shape of the circle. Keep a fairly light contact on the inside rein, and just squeeze it with a subtle opening and closing of your fingers – this will encourage the horse to accept the contact, rather than setting himself against it.

Achieving even modest success in dealing with this problem is evidence that you are becoming an effective rider. If you encounter it, compare what happens when you ride the same horse on circles in the opposite direction – you may find that he then tries to cut in! As I've said elsewhere, most horses are crooked through the body to some extent. Noticing things like this and comparing the physique and attitude of one horse to another is part and parcel of developing your knowledge and versatility as a rider.

Two Lateral Exercises

There are a number of exercises or movements in riding that have a sideways as well as a forward element. These are intended to benefit the training and gymnastic development of the horse, but learning how to do them also helps the rider to understand more about how the horse moves, and to apply the aids more thoughtfully, accurately and effectively. Most of these exercises are encountered at a more advanced stage than is covered by this book, but there are two that are often taught to riders at quite an early stage, one reason being that they help the rider become more proficient at getting the horse to respond to pressure from the leg. These exercises are called leg-yielding and turn on the forehand.

Leg-yielding

In leg-yielding, the horse moves to some extent diagonally (forwards and sideways simultaneously), the legs on the 'inside' of his body (the side *to* which he is slightly flexed and *away* from which he is moving) stepping over across the legs on his 'outside'). The greater the angle (the more sideways element) asked for, the more difficult the exercise. Horses can leg-yield in walk, trot and canter but, when pupils are first introduced to it, this will be in walk.

Instructors commonly start by asking pupils to leg-yield from the inside track (about 5 m in from the school wall) to the outside track. So, for example, in a 40 x 20 m school, you might be asked to turn from a short side up the three-quarter line and, starting from level with the M marker, leg-yield to the left so that you reach the outside track at F. (If you are going to leg-yield to the right, all the aids and directions that follow will, of course, be reversed.) Finishing at a specific marker (in this case, F) may seem demanding, but it actually helps to develop precision by giving a specific aim.

The aids are quite simple – to do this example of leg-yielding to the left, start with a good, active walk and a nice rein contact and ride a smooth turn from the short side of the school onto the three-quarter line.

Leg-yielding from the three-quarter line to the outside track. The small image shows how the horse steps forward and sideways in response to the rider's aids.

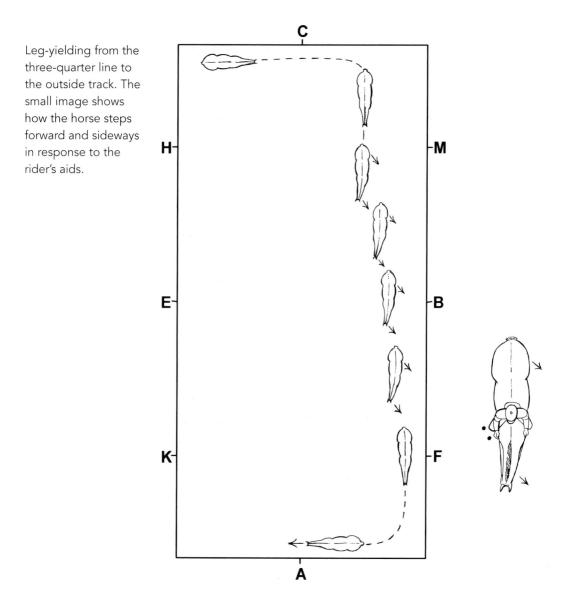

As you draw level with M, squeeze with your right hand to produce just a *slight* flexion of the horse's head towards the right then, sitting straight and looking ahead, apply pressure with your right leg to ask the horse to step over to the left with his own legs.

As with all new exercises, it may take some time and practise to get things right and your instructor will give tips on how to co-ordinate the aids to get the required result. These may include:

• Whether or not you need to move your right (inside) leg back a little.

- How to 'time' the leg aids so that they 'ask' when the horse's legs are in a position that allows him to respond (he can't 'step over' with his inside legs if they are already 'over').

- Whether you need to use your left (outside) leg (which will otherwise be resting against the horse's side) to help maintain the 'forward' part of the movement.

One of the advantages of introducing leg-yielding *towards* the outside track is the fact that the school walls have a 'magnetic' attraction for the horse, and he will tend to move quite readily in that direction. However, this can sometimes be a disadvantage because, especially if he is a bit lazy or the rider's aids are not very clear, the horse may just think: 'Oh, I'm supposed to go to the wall', and just drift over there anyhow. Since the essence of a correct leg-yield is that the horse's body remains parallel to any line he is aimed at, and that he gets there by steps that involve crossing his legs, 'drifting' doesn't fit the bill.

Although it can be harder to 'get the horse going' in the opposite direction, a rider may sometimes achieve a more technically correct leg-yield when asking the horse to move *away* from the track towards the three-quarter line. At some stage, a wise instructor will doubtless suggest this exercise because, other considerations apart, success suggests that the pupil's co-ordination and control of the horse are improving.

Another development of leg-yielding that can be of great value to riders is to leg-yield the horse out on a corner. Many school horses have a tendency to try to cut corners, 'leaning' into them with their inside shoulder, and riders often make the mistake of trying to 'hold' them out on the corner with the inside rein. (Why this is a mistake that doesn't work is explained in the section on Circling – turns through corners usually being a quarter of a circle.) In this exercise, designed to instil confidence in an effective method of control, the rider deliberately rides the corner 'short' and as the arc of a large circle. For instance, on the right rein, rather than passing the F marker on the way towards A, and trying to ride quite deep through the corner onto the short side, the rider deliberately turns onto a big arc a couple of metres before F. (For this exercise to be effective, the horse does need to have a correct bend in his body – in this example, to the right – but this should be quite easy to achieve because, on a big arc, this bend need only be slight and, if the horse was thinking of 'leaning' through the corner, he would have anticipated

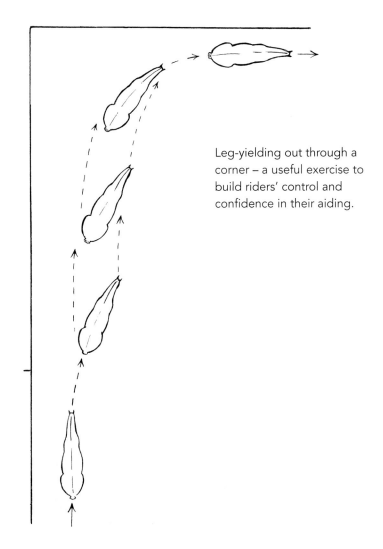

Leg-yielding out through a corner – a useful exercise to build riders' control and confidence in their aiding.

doing so once he was deeper into it.) A couple of strides into the arc the rider, sitting upright, uses significant pressure of the inside (in this case, right) leg to push the horse outwards towards the corner of the school. What they are then doing is riding the horse correctly from the inside leg into the outside rein.

Turn on the Forehand

Basically, this is just one means by which a horse can turn to face in a different direction: he does it by pivoting round one of his forelegs (the right foreleg if turning to face the right), hence 'the forehand'. There are various reasons for teaching the horse to do it under saddle (one of which is that it can assist a rider in the opening and closing of gates); the main reasons for teaching it to a rider are to emphasise the usefulness of a sideways-pushing leg aid and to improve overall co-ordination of the aids.

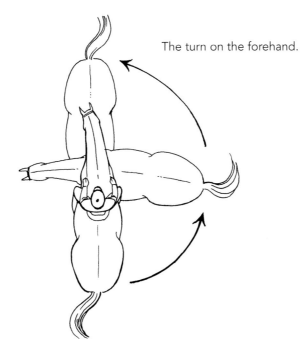

The turn on the forehand.

The horse needs some room to make this turn: it can't be ridden on the outside track because, depending on which way he turned, the horse would bang either his backside or his head on the school wall. Therefore, it needs to be started somewhere to the inside of the school. Although it can be ridden anywhere that offers *sufficient* room, instructors commonly introduce the exercise by putting pupils onto a track a couple of metres inside the outside track, and getting them to turn the horse's head towards the school perimeter. The reasoning behind this is that starting off *quite near* the school wall discourages the horse from trying to step forward when asked to turn. This is fine so long as the intention is to turn the horse through at least 180 degrees; an instructor who believes that a lesser turn will suffice for the first time of asking will probably start pupils off on a three-quarter line.

The movement is introduced following a halt from an active walk. Since it will help greatly if the halt itself is pretty much square, sensible instructors won't introduce this exercise until their pupils have become

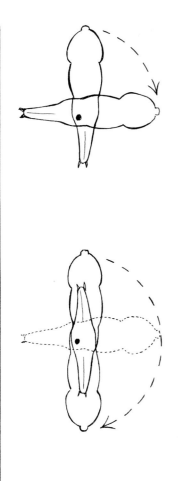

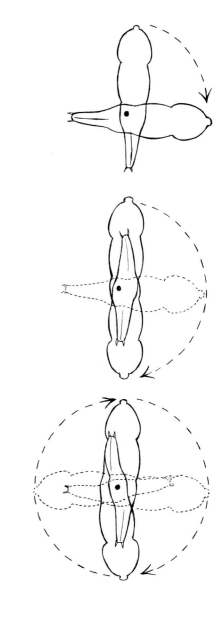

Turns on the forehand through 90 and 180 degrees, performed a couple of metres in from the arena wall. These diagrams show that, if these turns were attempted on the outside track, the horse wouldn't have room for his head and neck. However, by making the turn *quite close* to the wall, the horse is discouraged from stepping forwards.

Quarter-, half- and full turns on the forehand on the three-quarter line.

reasonably proficient at riding halts. The turn itself is best made as soon as the halt is established, while the horse is still attentive to the rider. As with leg-yielding, the reins retain a contact and the hand on the side towards which the horse's head is to turn (let's say, to the right, *see* the box below) gives a squeeze to indicate direction. Although the aim is to turn the horse's head to the right, this rein *does not haul* in that direction – the chief guiding aid comes from the rider's inside (in this case, right) leg, which comes back a little behind the girth and nudges the hindquarters to the left in a pulsing effect, step by step. This leg should not just give a protracted shove – the horse must be given time to take each individual step and it should be possible to dictate the angle through which the horse turns by asking for the number of steps necessary. (Usually, about four good steps will turn the horse through 90 degrees.) While the rider's inside leg produces this sideways stepping, the outside leg (left, in this example) generally rests quietly against the horse's side, but it can be used actively to give a correctional 'forward' aid if the horse tries to step backwards. Other than giving the initial 'suggestion' of direction, the rider's hands should generally retain just a quiet rein contact but, if the horse tries to step forward, they can give a retaining squeeze. Once the horse has turned the required amount, he should be ridden straight forward.

Although experienced school horses should not be unduly one-sided, most horses still have a residual 'preferred side' and you may notice that most horses will perform this turn a little more easily to one side than the other.

Once you have got the hang of leg-yielding and turns on the forehand, you will be more confident about the use of your inside leg and will feel more in control of the horse generally, but especially when riding turns and circles.

> Most people, including most BHS-trained instructors, will call this a 'right turn on the forehand', because the horse's head turns towards the right. However, there are some people who would call this a 'left turn on the forehand' because the horse's hindquarters turn to the left.

PART 5

Snippets

> This section contains some information and ideas that may be of interest and generally useful as you progress with your riding.

Why the Funny Handshake?

This is just a point of interest really, but many beginners are curious about the way they're told to hold the reins – i.e. coming into the hand between the little finger and the fourth finger. It dates back to the time when many horses were ridden in double bridles – two bits in the mouth and two sets of reins. There are several different ways to hold two sets of reins but, since it is desirable to produce individual actions from the two bits, this entails some separation of the reins, by the way in which they were held. One way of doing this is to have the bradoon rein coming into the hand above the little finger. The bradoon, the upper bit in the horse's mouth, is shaped and functions like a smaller, lighter version of a snaffle – the kind of bit most commonly used nowadays, especially for novice horses and riders. As it became standard practice to ride more horses just in snaffles, this way of holding the single reins became the norm (although it is not universal – quite a few jockeys, and some showjumpers, do hold the reins 'full fist').

Tradition aside, one advantage of holding the reins like this is that, because they are not in the whole fist, there is a tendency for riders (albeit a subconscious one) to use them more sensitively. Some instructors take this a step further, occasionally doing exercises in sensitivity in which they ask pupils to hold the reins in other ways (e.g. with two fingers each side).

A more detailed explanation of what holding the reins entails is given in Rein Contact.

Musical Horses

Physical compatibility permitting, most riding schools like their clients to experience riding a selection of horses. This can be a little disconcerting for some people at first, if they've just 'got used' to one horse and find they've been switched to another. However (assuming that all the horses used are basically suitable for beginners), the school has got it right – learning to 'tune in' to a variety of horses is a valuable part of the process. Now, there may be a temporary downside to this – you may find that you struggle to come to terms with a particular horse and feel that you've 'gone backwards' from last week's lesson, but you shouldn't be downcast if this happens. Horses are all different, both physically and in their other characteristics, and every rider in the world (even the Olympic champions) finds some harder to ride than others. And, as with so much in life, it is often the case that we learn more from demanding situations. In our jobs, for example, we are likely to develop our inter-personal skills more when we *have* to establish a working relationship with someone we consider a bit odd and not very likeable, than when we're working with someone affable and easy-going. That's not to say that we shouldn't enjoy working with nice people and riding nice horses, it's just that dealing with the more idiosyncratic characters can bring out our communication skills and (a point I keep making) a large part of riding is effective communication.

And there's another point about this: *we* are all individuals too, and just because you saw someone else have a bit of a struggle with a particular horse last week, it doesn't necessarily follow that you will, too – it takes two to form a partnership. So, if you turn up expecting to ride good old Patch, and find you're down to ride Panic Button, don't despair – take a deep breath and get out there and surprise yourself.

Don't Take a 'Tow'

When teaching group lessons, instructors will often have pupils formed up as a 'ride' – the whole class walking or trotting round the school in formation, a horse's length or so apart. Usually, a working pupil (assisting the instructor) a slightly more experienced client rider, or someone on a particularly amenable horse, will be at the front ('leading file'). Astute instructors will get pupils performing some useful exercises based on this formation which encourage individual thoughts and actions on the part of the pupils. Examples would be the 'rear file' (the rider at the back) halting while the rest of the ride continues; certain individuals turning across the school while the rest of the ride goes on round the track, etc. However, if or when such exercises are not being carried out, and the whole class is going in 'ride' formation, there is a likelihood that both horses and riders (other than the leading file) will get a little lazy. What happens is that the horses, being herd animals, will just plod along behind the one in front and, knowing the drill, they will do things such as cutting corners if they find they are getting left behind a naturally faster or, longer-striding horse in front. This situation is made worse if the riders also 'switch off', simply allowing their horses to mooch along while they, themselves, take a mental and physical break.

For an inexperienced rider who has, perhaps, been working quite hard and has been given several things to think about, this might seem attractive, but the truth is, it is not riding; it is being a passenger. The point about riding is that the rider controls the horse – and being in a ride like this actually offers proactive riders the chance to practise their skills in a slightly challenging situation. If, when you are in the middle of a ride, you can go correctly through corners, rather than allowing your horse to cut them; if you can keep him trotting in the rhythm and speed *you* choose (see box on page 127); if you can halt in good time a length behind the horse in front rather than allowing your horse to barge (dangerously) into the other horse's hindquarters, you have achieved something worthwhile – so don't be content to 'take a tow'.

Obviously, if your horse is more active than some others in the ride, you can't just let him run into them on the basis that you 'wanted to keep him going'. Good instructors will explain that, in order to avoid any such problems, riders who find themselves too close to the horse in front should circle away to the inside of the school, and rejoin the ride where there is a suitable gap, or else take the rear file position. This riding a circle in isolation, and looking ahead for a suitable, safe gap is, of itself, a valuable exercise in control.

Fiddling with Your Straps

There may be times during a lesson when the length of your stirrup leathers needs adjusting. This is almost certain to happen in the early stages, when you are still trying to establish your basic position, and your instructor may lead the way in this respect, suggesting that they should be altered and helping with the process while you are at halt. However, as you progress, it is likely that you will make your own decisions in this respect, perhaps when riding a different horse for the first time and getting used to his shape and how he moves. (If the ground conditions in your school change with the weather, this may also influence how horses move, and you might find that you want to make minor adjustments to the leathers on a familiar horse, to take account of a slight change in his action.)

Whatever the reasons for adjusting the leathers, some riders – even of several years experience – continue to view it as a Herculean task, wandering around in the middle of the school for half a millennium with slack reins, one foot out of the stirrup and the leather over their thigh, while they peer down and fumble with the buckle. Apart from being unnecessary (see box on page 128), this process could be potentially dangerous in some situations and, once you are past the total beginner stage it is a good idea to practise adjusting your leathers swiftly and without fuss, while you are still in motion. Some instructors will teach you how to do it, but the basic process, which relies on using the weight of your leg, is as follows:

1 Remaining looking ahead, take both reins in the hand you are not going to use to adjust the first leather.

2 Ease the leg on the side of the leather you are about to adjust away from the horse's side.

3 Reach down, locate the buckle on the leather and, with your thumb and forefinger, remove the buckle tongue out of its existing hole. If you want to lengthen the leather, ease a little more weight of your leg into the stirrup, 'feel' the leather down a hole and refasten the buckle. If you want to shorten the leather, keep just sufficient weight in the stirrup to hold the leather taut while you draw it up a hole and refasten.

4 Change hands and repeat on the other side.

With a little practice, you will find that you can do this almost without thinking while the horse remains at walk.

> There are some saddles with deeply recessed stirrup bars (the bars by which the leathers are attached to the saddle) that make adjustment rather fiddly, but these are quite rare, especially on the types of saddle commonly used in riding schools.

If you use the right procedure, adjusting your stirrup leathers is a straightforward process.

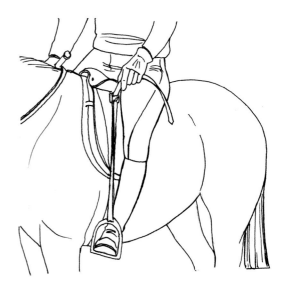

Uses of a Whip

The Whip as an Aid

The principal use of the whip is not to punish the horse, but to support the leg aids. For this reason, the following section should be considered in conjunction with Using Your Legs and all other text in Part 2 that relates to the general principles of applying the aids.

There is a certain paradox in the horse's physiology: although, compared to a human, he has quite a thick skin, he has many nerve endings in it that are very sensitive to touch. It is this sensitivity to feel that is the basis of correct use of the whip. Although it might sound strange, the sensation of quite a light slap with the whip, concentrated on a small area, will produce more response from a horse than a rider's legs thumping dully against his sides. Therefore, at times when a horse is 'hard work' and needs to be made rather more responsive to the leg aids, a timely tap can serve to wake him up. In addition to being effective, it will also be far less unpleasant for the horse than a repeated drumming of boots against his lower ribs.

There is a general principle of applying all aids that they should, ideally, be as light as is effective, and this also applies to using the whip. No decent person wants to hit a horse unnecessarily, or unnecessarily hard.

The basic indicator of when it might be necessary to use the whip is when you've given an aid with your legs and got an inadequate response (the horse is more or less ignoring you). In this case, the procedure is to repeat the leg aid, reinforcing it with a simultaneous use of the whip, just behind the leg. 'Leg' (singular) here will normally apply to your inside leg: when riding in a school, it is generally the horse's inside hind leg that needs to be activated to maintain forward impulse and balance. This being so, it is necessary to switch your whip from one hand to the other whenever you change direction, and we'll look at this further when discussing the different types of whip.

Precisely how hard the whip should be applied for optimum effect will vary a little depending on the horse and the circumstance. However, many people err on the side of 'being kind' to the extent they literally do no more than tickle the horse. This is counter-productive because the whole purpose of using the whip is to produce an immediate response: if a horse is ignoring your legs, you don't then want him to ignore the whip as well. Your instructor should tell you whether your use of the whip is appropriate but, as a general principle, if you start off by being moderately firm you should then find that the horse will respond to a lighter use on any subsequent occasion – this is much preferable to finding that you have to keep using the whip harder.

Another aspect of using the whip is that it's illogical (and unfair to the horse) to give an instruction and then countermand it. If you use the whip to demand more activity from the horse, it's a nonsense if you don't then allow this activity because your reins are restricting the forward movement. So, the way in which you handle and use the whip should not, of itself, cause the rein contact to increase.

Using the whip whilst, at the same time, restricting forward movement is nonsensical.

Types of whip

There are two basic forms of whip that can be used for general riding and the fundamental division between them is 'short' and 'long'.

Short whips There are different designs and names for such whips but they are most commonly known as jumping whips. These whips are generally about 2 ft 6 in in length, and have a padded flap at the business end and some sort of knob at the top of the handle to balance them and make them harder to drop. Whips significantly shorter than the length mentioned are pretty useless, as are cheap plastic ones that look like sticks of liquorice.

The advantages of a short whip lie in its versatility. Jumping riders use it because it can be switched readily from hand to hand and a well-timed slap with the flap can encourage a reluctant horse to make the required effort at an obstacle. It is a good type to carry when riding out, because its relative shortness means that it is less likely than a longer whip to get snagged on various obstructions, and its advantage for less experienced riders in the school is that it can be easier to change from hand to hand than a long whip (see below).

The disadvantage of a short whip is that it is harder to use than a long one for touching the horse's flank just behind the rider's leg, as a reinforcement for the leg aid – which, as mentioned earlier, is its key purpose. It certainly *can* be used in this way, but this involves taking the whip hand off the rein to avoid pulling the horse in the mouth, and this in turn entails switching that rein into the other hand. This is hard to do absolutely instantaneously and (unless the rider is experienced and very dextrous) entails some reduction in the quality of rein contact.

Long whips are usually called schooling whips, or dressage whips. They have a slim profile and, rather than a broad, flat flap, they have either a small, thin leather tongue, or end in a kind of plaited pigtail. Most such whips are about 3 ft 3 in (i.e. a metre) long, but some are longer, the very long ones being designed for experienced riders who may want to make subtle adjustments to the movement of a highly trained horse. These very long versions are unwieldy in all but expert hands and unnecessary in 'normal' riding situations.

Of limited value in other situations, the primary use for long whips is in the school, where their main advantage is that their length allows the rider to apply them with a flick of the wrist without taking a hand off the reins. This makes them much better for the purpose of reinforcing the leg aid than a short whip. Their potential disadvantage, especially for inexperienced riders, is that they can be quite unwieldy to switch from hand to hand – and it is really necessary to do this at each change of direction because a long whip in the outside hand is likely to rattle annoyingly along the school wall or fence, perhaps even bouncing back off it and giving the horse an unwarranted and irritating series of taps on his outside flank.

The correct way to use short and long whips.

Switching whip hand

To switch a short whip the procedure is: hand not holding whip transfers its rein into whip hand; free hand pulls whip upward out of whip hand and drops back to normal position; that hand, now holding whip, retakes its rein.

To switch a long whip the procedure is: free hand puts its rein into whip hand; free hand rolls over (thumb downwards) and takes hold of whip handle below current whip hand; free hand takes whip out of former whip hand and rolls back up (so that whip is pointed end up in front of rider); whip is then twirled round by the fingers of new whip hand so that, as it reaches its new side, it is once more pointed downwards; new whip hand then retakes its rein.

The latter, in particular, can seem like a sleight of hand trick at first and these changes are perhaps best demonstrated by the instructor and then practised at halt before they are attempted in motion. This reduces the chances of less dextrous pupils knocking their glasses off or going to Casualty to have a whip handle removed from their right nostril. (Although changes are not really *that* difficult, they may take a little practice.)

Whip Indications and Exercises

In addition to their primary function, whips can serve as indicators of what riders are doing with their hands. So long as the hands are in a reasonably correct position, the whip (of either design) will rest against the rider's thigh, pointing downwards and being angled somewhat backwards, towards the horse's flank. (From this position, a long whip can be applied accurately with just a flick of the rider's wrist.) A whip stuck out at some strange angle is clear evidence to an instructor that the pupil's hands are doing something untoward – and a whip wiggling about is clear evidence that the hand holding it is far from still.

As well as noting such errors in the hands, astute instructors sometimes incorporate whips into exercises they have devised to show up and improve errors of posture.

The Whip as Punishment

It would be unrealistic to say that, when riding, it is *never* necessary or justifiable to use the whip for punishment. However, doing so justifiably presupposes that the rider has correctly assessed some action (or inaction) on the horse's part as blatant disobedience. In such cases, if it is to be effective, any use of the whip must be virtually instantaneous, otherwise the horse won't be able to connect the punishment with his behaviour. What is required in such circumstances is one sharp smack *immediately* the disobedience becomes evident, then to continue as though nothing had happened.

But so far as novice riders are concerned:

1 In a horse suitable for a beginner, any behaviour deserving of actual punishment (as opposed to the occasional, 'Oi, listen' tap) should be a real rarity.

2 If a horse *does* exhibit real disobedience, few beginners have developed sufficient speed of thought and action to respond quickly enough in the first instance for any punishment to be effective.

3 Simply through inexperience, beginners may misinterpret a horse's action (or lack of it). That is, they may think a horse is being disobedient when he simply doesn't understand what is being asked of

him. In such circumstances, any punishment would be unjust and counter-productive.

For these reasons, it is better for novice riders not to think about using the whip for punishment without the specific say-so of the instructor. This, if it comes, is likely to be in the form of: 'That was a bit naughty – if he does it again, give him a smack immediately.' (In the unlikely event that you are told to punish the horse on any kind of regular basis, this would bring into query either the instructor's attitude or the horse's suitability as a mount for a beginner.)

Lunge Lessons

Having lessons on the lunge has long been considered an essential part of a rider's education in continental Europe and, indeed, many other places. It is still something of a rarity among beginners in the UK and may even be seen in certain quarters as 'a bit poncy' – something done by people who take it all too seriously. However, it is perhaps worth noting that the British, in general, have a casual attitude to doing most things that might improve their sporting performance. How many golf-playing friends do you know, who might benefit from regular professional instruction? Likely answer – all of them. And how many *have* these regular lessons?

Lungeing involves having a horse going in circles around the person in charge, at the end of a long lunge line. In addition to holding the lunge line, the person doing the lungeing also carries a long whip, which is used to encourage the horse forwards and to help fine-tune his gait and accuracy on the circle. Working a horse on the lunge can have many benefits to his schooling, and giving a rider exercises to do on the lunge can significantly improve their position. That is, provided that the person doing the lungeing is experienced and accomplished in the art, and that the horse being used is familiar with the process and can be relied upon to work rhythmically and obediently. If these criteria are not in place, the exercise will be of no value, and possibly counter-productive.

If your riding school offers lunge lessons, and you are happy that the instructor and the horse fit the bill, then a few such lessons can be enormously helpful in improving your posture and security. The key point about lunge lessons is that, since it is the instructor who takes full control of the horse, the pupil can concentrate entirely on these matters, without

Well-taught lunge lessons can do a lot to improve a rider's posture and security.

having to worry about keeping the horse going, or directing him. In fact, it is usual for a pupil on the lunge not to have access to the reins; the hands and arms being free to perform posture-enhancing exercises. (If it becomes necessary to hold anything, the pupil grasps the front of the saddle which – as we've seen elsewhere, is a vastly more useful aid to security than hanging on to the reins.) This 'hands free' approach has another, subtle but important benefit, that perhaps has even more impact if lunge lessons are taken at an early stage: the rider becomes more aware of communicating with the horse through seat and legs, and less reliant upon the hands – a state of affairs that would be desirable in most riders. Another, straightforward, advantage is that, since lunge lessons are necessarily one-to-one, all of the instructor's focus is on you. For this, and other reasons, lunge lessons are quite intensive, and they will be considerably shorter in duration than a standard one hour class lesson; they will also work out more expensive on a time-for-time basis. However, because of their intensity and focus, they can still represent very good value for money in terms of your progress.

Helping to Tack Up

Patently, when you first turn up at the riding school, you will not be expected to help tack up – i.e. fit the saddle and bridle to the horse you are going to ride. This is for the very obvious reasons that you may be unfamiliar with handling horses, and you won't know how to fit things in a way that is comfortable for the horse and safe for you. However, as you look round the yard you may see this process being carried out, and start to wonder what is involved.

In due course, becoming more familiar with handling horses and knowing something about tack and its correct adjustment can be very beneficial. In the first instance, the more you can get 'up close and personal' with the horse in his own space, the more you will learn about him as an animal, and this can only help with regard to how you think from his perspective and communicate with him in the saddle. The second point is that, in addition to involving you with handling horses, understanding the basics of tack and its fitting will make you more aware of things that might compromise your safety in a different environment. For example, if, in due course, you decide to have a holiday ride at a centre unfamiliar to you, it is worth knowing enough to notice whether saddlery stitching is badly worn, whether girths, stirrup leathers or reins need replacing, whether the bit seems not to fit, etc.

Most good schools will welcome interest in these matters from pupils, and it will be well worthwhile getting to the school a few minutes before your lesson time to watch and learn whilst horses are being made ready. Some schools, in fact, run stable management lessons, which teach the basics, not only of tacking up, but also of subjects such as grooming, shoeing, feeding, etc. Such lessons will be very helpful to anyone who just wants to know more about horses, and of particular interest to anyone with long-term ambitions to have their own.

PART 6

Out and About

> This section deals with riding beyond the confines
> of the school.

Riding Out

The chance to ride a horse out in the open (traditionally known as 'hacking', or 'going for a hack') is one of the main reasons why many people take up riding in the first place. For reasons that should be obvious by now, responsible schools teach the rudiments of riding in an enclosed area initially, but most offer pupils the chance to ride out when they feel that they have reached a sufficient level of competence.

I should say at this point that variety in riding is of great benefit to both horses and riders. As human beings we are all individuals and, whatever sporting and leisure activities we take part in, we will inevitably develop preferences for some aspects over others. Anglers may prefer rivers to lakes; tennis players singles to doubles; theatre-goers Shaw to Shakespeare – or whatever. In the same way, some riders may be more captivated by the prospect of polishing their technique within the confines of the school; others by the prospect of viewing the countryside from horseback and having a canter across the heath. As skills increase, these preferences may be reflected in a chosen discipline – showjumping, dressage, endurance riding, etc. However, while such preferences are a fact of life and the individual's choice, anyone who wishes to develop their basic riding skills to a reasonable level would be well-advised to practise both what the Continentals used to call 'interior' and 'exterior' riding – they are, in fact, complementary.

I hope that much of what I've said earlier will have helped new-comers, who perhaps got into riding simply with thoughts of 'going for a mooch around the common', to realise that it makes sense to learn the basics first – both in terms of safety and the increased enjoyment born of a degree of competence. However, the studious rider who wants to keep concentrating on school work on the assumption: 'That's where I'll learn most' will be surprised how much can be learnt when riding out, on a horse who is in his natural environment, in company.

How a riding school introduces riding out will depend upon its general philosophy and the surrounding environment. A school that has suitable land of its own may introduce short rides round its own fields as an interim measure, perhaps as the second half of a lesson. In many cases, however, the only areas available will be land with public rights of access, and getting to it may entail some riding on public roads. When riding out:

1 So far as is practical, pupils should have their first experience on horses they have previously ridden and got on well with in school lessons.

2 There must be an experienced adult member of staff (ideally, at first, the pupils' usual instructor) acting as chief escort. If there are more than a handful of pupils (and/or it is necessary to ride on public roads) the school should provide one or more additional competent riders to assist the chief escort.

3 A thorough check of tack should always be made before setting off.

From the school's point of view (as well as the horses'), it is much better if horses can be ridden out on a regular basis – this both gives the horses a break from school work and makes going out more of a normal event. However, for various reasons, in many schools the amount of time horses spend out in the open is quite limited, certainly compared to most horses in private ownership. For this reason, when they do go out they can be a bit like kids on a school trip – out with their mates, doing something different from the everyday routine. As a consequence, they may be rather keener and livelier than they would be plodding round the school, on their third lesson of the day. That is not to say that horses used for a novice hack are likely to be badly behaved – but they will, perhaps, be sufficiently perkier than usual for their riders to notice the difference.

Three Tips

Here are some tips that may be useful when you start to venture out of the school:

1 If you are likely to be riding over any uneven ground – e.g. if the local terrain is rather hilly, or the ground is likely to be muddy – it is a good idea, before you set out, to shorten your stirrup leathers one hole from how you would have them for riding in the school. This will help you to retain your stirrups if your horse suffers any slight loss of balance, for example stumbling over a tree root whilst trotting. It will also increase your sense of security if, for instance, you have to duck or lean sideways to avoid protruding branches.

2 So long as it is safe to do so (i.e. traffic conditions permit) try to avoid your horse stepping on any drain or manhole covers – these can be quite slippery, especially when wet.

3 Don't let your horse grab mouthfuls of food. This may be understandable from his view, but it's bad manners. While he's trying to grab cow parsley from the hedgerow, he won't be concentrating on you, and that's no good if the horse in front stops suddenly, or an articulated lorry comes round the corner in the middle of the road. This is one time when you can respond to his actions with a brief tug on the opposite rein and a kick against his sides, to send the message, 'Oi, greedy guts – focus on me.' Bad manners aside, some plants are poisonous to horses and (despite what some people may tell you) horses *don't* always have the instinctive good sense to avoid them.

If, on grassland, your horse tries to put his head down to eat, *don't* try to pull it back up with your arms – this isn't good for either his mouth or your back. Instead, give him a sharp kick with your legs – he should respond by raising his head and stepping forward. If, following that, he again eyes up the grass and starts to reach down, a pre-emptive squeeze should do the trick.

If your horse tries to stick his head down to eat (*top left*), don't respond by trying to pull it back up with your arms (*top right*); instead, apply your legs strongly (*right*).

Road Sense

In many areas nowadays (although riding schools are always keen to keep this to a practical minimum) it is impossible to reach open spaces without riding on public roads. While it is the responsibility of the escort(s) to ensure the overall safety of the ride, the individual riders also have a responsibility to act in a way that makes this task as easy as possible. Also, in the final analysis, it is only the person on the horse who can exercise direct control over him. Therefore, when riding on the road, you should always:

- Ride with care, full attention and to the best of your ability.

- Comply with all instructions from the escorting rider(s).

- Keep to your allotted position in the ride. In particular, maintain the prescribed distance (usually a horse's length) between your horse and the horse in front – straggling, especially, can cause serious problems if drivers try to 'slot in' or come out of side roads between elements of a ride.

- Draw prompt attention to anything which affects your ability to carry out either of the preceding two points.

- Acknowledge any courtesy shown by another road user. (If you don't fancy taking a hand off the rein to raise it, just nod or smile.)

Riding school horses used for novice hacks should be familiar with traffic and various other local sights and sounds, and thus as well-behaved and safe on the roads as can be practically expected of a horse. However, the fact remains that horses retain their instincts and the possibility exists that *any* horse may, on occasion, be confronted by something he finds worrying. I'm not going to alarm you here by inventing bizarre and improbable scenarios, but there's one tip that can be of practical use in circumstances that are not uncommon.

In Britain, where we drive, and thus ride, on the left side of the road, it is 'spooky' objects on that side that most concern us. (Readers in countries which drive on the right should mentally reverse the points made below.) If the object is on the right then, in most circumstances, there is room to pass it safely – the horse may have a look but, with encouragement from the rider, he will be willing enough to pass by. However, if a horse is worried by an object on the left, his instinct will be to move away from it – i.e. further out into the road. Since, potentially, this means stepping into the path of traffic, the instinct of many riders is to try to pull him back over with the left rein. But, as we saw earlier (Showing, not Steering), if a horse's head is pulled one way, his back end will tend to swing in the opposite direction. So, in this situation, pulling a horse's head to the left creates two problems. The first is that it will tend to turn him side-on across the road, with his back end out in the middle; the second is that he will now be head-on (and close to) the thing that is frightening him – and one of his possible reactions to this will be to step *backwards*. So, in attempting to solve a problem, this reaction by the rider has made it potentially much worse.

To avoid getting into this situation, there are two things you can do:

1 Always to be alert to anything on the near side of the road that might alarm a horse. In saying this, I'm not suggesting that you should proceed in a permanent state of anxiety – simply that a moment's warning gives you some time to take the appropriate action. (In practice, the leading escort should notice anything that might be cause for concern, and warn the ride but, as I've said elsewhere, learning to think for oneself is always an asset to a rider.)

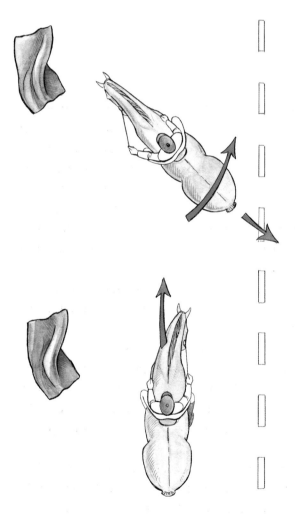

Wrong and right ways of dealing with a spooky object. *Top:* the horse's instinct is to step further away from the object and the rider's instinct is to try to keep him close to it by pulling on the left rein. However, this has caused the horse's hindquarters to swing outward, turning him nearly side-on and, if he now 'backs off', he will be stepping backwards into the middle of the road. *Bottom:* the rider has turned the horse's head away from the object and is using strong pressure from the right leg both to hold the horse's hindquarters in and encourage him past it.

2 So long as traffic conditions are such that it is safe to attempt to pass the object (again, in practice, the escort will make the judgement on this), you should ride in a way that is more or less a reversal of the error described above. In addition to giving the object as wide a berth as is safe, you should take a stronger contact on the *right* rein (so that the horse's head is turned slightly away from the object) and, moving your right leg a little behind the girth, apply strong pressure to dissuade him from swinging his back end out into the road. Your legs, aided by reassurance from your voice, encourage the horse to move promptly past the problem.

This positioning is a rather crude form of an exercise called shoulder-in, which is used in the school for the gymnastic benefit of the horse.

Cantering in the Open

We have already talked about starting to canter and, by the time you venture out for a ride in the open, you should have reached a stage in your lessons at which you are riding regularly in canter for short periods. So long as a school is happy that riders have reached such a level, they will usually try, where appropriate, to include a period or two of canter during the ride. Done judiciously, this should be great fun for the riders – a brisk, free canter in the open is one of the joys of riding. However, there are potential constraints that must be taken into consideration by both instructors and pupils.

In the first instance, there are times when conditions are simply unsuitable for cantering. If the ground is hard and rutted (either in the aftermath of freezing weather, or in a long hot spell), cantering may cause lameness in the horses. Alternatively, excessively deep, sticky mud may pull tendons, pull off shoes, or cause horses (especially those ridden by novices) to become unbalanced. The horses' welfare and the safety of horses and riders must always be paramount – so never be too disappointed if the instructor says that cantering is not feasible on a particular day.

One problem faced by many schools is limited access to riding country generally, and to places where cantering can be done safely in particular. Since horses are creatures of habit, this can lead to them knowing where the regular canter tracks are, and thus anticipating the canter. This can cause them to become rather over-eager – which in turn can make things a little awkward for both instructor and pupils.

When exercising horses, sensible private owners will make sure that they don't always ask their horses to canter or gallop in the same place: sometimes, they will make a point of walking or trotting along what is more often a 'canter' stretch, and do their fast work elsewhere. This is valuable training, because it helps teach the horse to listen to the rider, rather than getting the idea that he can make his own decisions. It could be said that this principle is even more important when dealing with riding school horses, and astute instructors with a choice of canter tracks will no doubt apply it. Those who don't have much choice may also try to put the principle into effect by saying, on occasion: 'We'll just trot along here today.' Riders who have become used to enjoying a canter may be disappointed by this, but in fact, they will learn more from keeping in trot horses who are expecting to canter than they will from just watching the scenery whiz by. And this brings us to the matter of control.

Now, I don't want to alarm you by suggesting that when a group of riders canter in the open they are *likely* to be out of control. In fact, shortly, I'm going to suggest why the opposite is not only desirable but should be easily achievable. However, to emphasise why control is important, let's look at things from the instructor's point of view.

When an instructor intends to let a group of riders have a canter, there are two basic options: they can either do so in line abreast, or in single file. In some situations, the formation may be dictated by circumstances – if the only track available is quite narrow, then clearly riders can't all canter up it side by side. However, both options have potential drawbacks:

If a number of horses are cantering line abreast:

1 They may tend to 'race'.

2 If riders cannot keep good control of direction and a safe distance apart, horses may get too close together, in which case one may, through excitement or a 'keep out of my space' attitude, kick out sideways and injure another horse, or his rider. Other than this, horses may simply collide, and one may barge another onto unsuitable ground.

If a number of horses are cantering in single file:

1 When they see others cantering off, horses who are having to wait may become fidgety and start jumping around which, in a confined space, can be potentially dangerous. Novice riders may also find it difficult to keep excited horses in check.

2 In single file, a faster/longer-striding horse behind a slower one may, if not fully controlled, run dangerously up the backside of the horse in front.

Precisely how an instructor chooses to deal with these issues depends on a number of factors, including the actual terrain, availability of assistants (escorts) and knowledge of the individual horses and their riders' abilities. However, the real key to avoiding problems lies in the riders' control.

Now, for any particularly gung-ho readers, I should emphasise that I'm not suggesting that horses having a canter on the common should mince along as though they were in shackles – on the contrary, both they, and their riders, should thoroughly enjoy themselves. However, this is much more likely to happen if riders *are* exercising a reasonable degree of control because:

- Being in control is evidence of having learnt a skill. (There is no skill in just going fast; the skill lies in going fast *under control* – ask any Formula 1 driver.)

- Unless you are a borderline insane adrenalin junkie, being in control is inherently more enjoyable than being out of control.

- Being in control instils confidence in the rider, who is then likely to enjoy going incrementally faster as experience and circumstances permit.

- A confident rider, who is enjoying the experience, won't yank at the reins and 'fight' the horse, as a rider who feels out of control may do – so the experience is much more enjoyable for the horse.

- Riders who are in control are much more likely to avoid distinctly unpleasant experiences, such as running over a child or dog who has run out from the bushes, or trampling another rider who has had the misfortune to fall off.

When cantering in the open, you, your horse, and probably anyone in your company will enjoy the experience more if you can avoid looking like the upper picture and look more like the lower picture. This can be achieved by understanding how to adapt your posture.

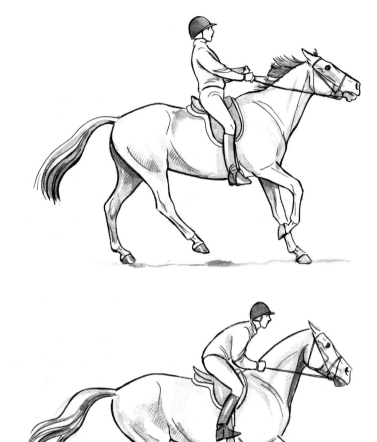

Posture

So, what are the key elements for controlling a horse at speed in the open? The most significant one is the rider's posture. We saw earlier (Posture, not Posing) how important posture is to effective riding, and we've looked at the key elements of this in the context of riding in the school. We've also seen one example (see Rising Trot) of why it is sometimes expedient to adapt the basic posture to take account of different conditions, and when cantering in the open it is likely (although not inevitable) that one or more of the following conditions will apply:

1 The cantering takes place over less even terrain and for considerably further than would be the case in the school.

2 Both rider and horse want to go faster than in the school.

3 The horse, perhaps through the stimulus of cantering in company, or simply wishing to 'let his hair down' in a natural environment, wants to go faster than the rider does.

(I should make the point that *if* the canter is to be fairly short, on fairly level ground, at a moderate speed *and* the horse has no inclination to go faster than the rider wishes – or, if he does have this inclination, the rider senses this is and has sufficient skill to keep the horse fully 'on the aids' and under control – then it is perfectly possible to canter in the open in the same way as in the school – in which case, nothing need change. However, as stated, this combination of circumstances is not typical of cantering in the open.)

So, how do we deal with these variables? What is needed, ideally, is a posture that will ease the horse's task when you want him to stride on, but can be adapted quickly to restrain him if it becomes necessary to do so.

With regard to the first point, this has something in common with the original reasons for rising to the trot – easing the horse's back and the rider's backside when going for long journeys over rough ground. Of course, I'm not suggesting that (in the early stages at any rate) you will be cantering for miles on end, nor am I suggesting that you should do 'rising canter'. What I am suggesting is a kind of 'poised' canter – if your weight is kept just off the saddle, this makes things easier and more comfortable for the horse over uneven ground and it allows the big muscles in his back to transfer the thrust from his hind legs more efficiently. This also helps to make it easier for the horse to go faster *in accordance with the rider's wishes*.

But this is not just a matter of 'getting off the horse's back' – being in balance with him is important, too, and this brings us to consider the horse's *centre of gravity*.

In a body capable of independent movement and changes of balance (such as a horse) the centre of gravity is not a fixed point. However, its *approximate general* location in a horse will be vertically beneath his spine at a point a little in front of a normally seated rider's knee and, as he stretches out in the faster gaits, it may move further forward. If you want a horse to travel at speed with as little effort as possible, it will help not only if you take your weight off his back, but if you place it as nearly as possible over (but never in front of) his centre of gravity which – given its general location in relation of your 'normal' (fully seated) posture – will require you to fold your upper body forwards.

At this point, you may recall the warnings in Posture, not Posing about the drawbacks of leaning forward in the fork seat, or curling forward in the foetal position – and rightly so. Attempting to ride at speed in these positions would be highly precarious – especially if the horse stumbled – and if he tried to speed up against your will, you would have precious little chance of preventing this – so these postures are *not* what I am suggesting. In order to produce a secure basis for a forward-folded posture, what is needed is an enhanced 'platform of balance' which, as its name suggests, is something that provides a degree of mechanical security.

When you sit on a horse in a normally correct posture, your platform of balance is pretty much provided by the front-to-rear distance of your seat bones. *So long as you are sitting upright*, this is quite sufficient for normal riding on the flat but, once your upper body moves significantly

The curled forward foetal position is always to be avoided, but especially when riding at speed, when it will offer virtually nothing in the way of security or control.

forward, this platform is too narrow to maintain your equilibrium (which is one reason why the fork seat and foetal position – in which your platform of balance is pretty much limited to the front of your seat bones – are so insecure). You can prove this to yourself when sitting without stirrups on a horse at halt – see how far you can fold your upper body forward without losing balance or gripping fiercely with your legs.

What's needed, then, is a wider platform of balance, which will support you as you fold forward further, and this is achieved by shortening your stirrup leathers. The result of this is that the angles of your knees and hips are closed and your thighs move upwards and forwards, and it is this altered thigh position which increases the platform of balance. Again, you can prove this to yourself at halt, adjusting the stirrup leathers to various lengths and seeing how far you can fold forward in balance. The shorter the leathers, the wider the platform of balance, but there is a

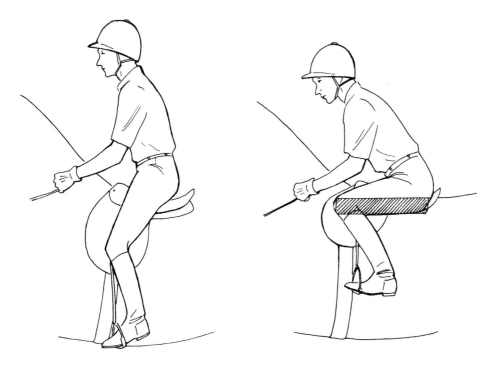

When you want to ride in a forward seat, having your stirrup leathers at their normal length (*left*) offers a platform of balance that is undesirably narrow. Shortening your leathers (*right*) alters the angle of your thighs and provides a much wider platform of balance (*shaded*). (The leathers of the right-hand rider are shown shortened beyond what would normally be necessary for novice riders on school horses to emphasise the point.)

trade-off for most things and *very* short leathers (see box below) place great strain on the leg muscles, will make riders unused to them feel insecure and, for the purpose of making it easy for the average riding school horse to have a nice, free canter, they are simply unnecessary. All that's required is an adjustment sufficient to enable you to remain poised just clear of the saddle, so that your backside doesn't bump into it at every canter stride. This fulfils the requirement to keep your weight 'off the horse's back' and it should also provide a platform of balance sufficient to enable you to fold forward in harmony with the horse whilst maintaining a secure position. It is hard to say precisely how many holes you will need to shorten your leathers to achieve this position, because this depends on various factors including your normal length of leathers for flatwork, your conformation, the horse's conformation and the style of saddle you are using. However, as a starting point, you should think of shortening them just a couple of holes. Later on, if you progress to riding faster, stronger horses at gallop, you will probably want to shorten your leathers more, but on most riding school horses this should be unnecessary – and too big an adjustment, too soon, may *feel* strange and insecure.

I made the point earlier (First Sensations in the Saddle) that we humans are very sensitive to changes from what we have learnt to consider 'the norm' and even this apparently modest alteration in the length of stirrup leathers can seem quite odd (even unwelcome) to some riders – until they have got used to it and felt the benefits when riding at speed. To develop familiarity, it is good practice (although seemingly not that common) for instructors to give pupils the chance to get used to the 'feel' of riding for brief periods with shortened leathers in the school before attempting to do so in open spaces.

Of course, jockeys ride *very* short, but they are alternating between having to exercise maximum control over a racehorse travelling very fast in close proximity to other horses (running into the back of another horse at racing pace can be *extremely* dangerous) and trying to assist the horse to go absolutely flat out. Their postures are examples of the same principles we are discussing, but taken to extremes to cope with exceptional circumstances.

So, this folded-forward posture will make the process of cantering on easier for your horse and (like rising to the trot) you can adopt it as soon as he is settled into the gait. But what do you do if he is rather *too* enthusiastic? The answer to this lies in knowing a little about another 'centre' in the horse's body – the *centre of motion*. This, (in terms of its position in the horse's body) is a fairly static point: effectively the midway point along the spine between the fore and hind limbs. When a rider is sitting in a correct posture in a well-made saddle, the horse's centre of motion will be pretty much directly beneath the rider's lower spine – it is this juxtaposition that makes the seat and weight aids of an experienced rider so effective when doing normal work in the school (see also A Word About the Seat).

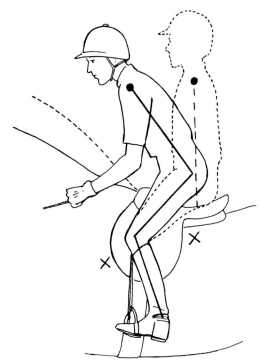

Appropriately shortened stirrup leathers allow for easy adjustments of the rider's posture when cantering in the open. *Solid figure* shows rider poised with seat out of the saddle and weight placed towards the horse's approximate centre of gravity – a posture that promotes ease and comfort for both horse and rider when the horse is settled into a rhythm and can be allowed to 'bowl along'. *Dotted figure* shows the rider's weight (with straight back) placed over the horse's centre of motion – a strong posture to adopt if the horse seems keen to quicken beyond the speed the rider requires.

If the horse is keener than required, moving your upper body back to the vertical will put your weight over his centre of motion, and the platform of balance formed by your shortened leathers should strengthen your position sufficiently to enable you either to 'hold' him at his current speed or to slow him down. If he is *very* keen, rather than returning your seat to the saddle it may be necessary to keep it just clear – in this way, you are steadying the horse with your weight and the big muscles of your thighs and back. Not only is this highly effective, it is also less uncomfortable for the horse than yanking away with your hands and socking him in the mouth with the bit. There are some supplementary points to add to this:

1 As always, the rider's response to the horse's actions should be proportionate. I'm not suggesting that, any time the horse is a little keen, you should lean back and throw your whole weight on the reins – use this change of posture in moderation and just as much as is necessary to steady the horse.

2 *As soon as* he responds by steadying, reward him by easing your posture – assuming that he steadies to the speed you require, you can revert to the poised posture that makes things easy and comfortable for him.

3 Any time a horse gets 'strong', in addition to your other responses, avoid taking a dead, heavy hold of the reins – that just gives him something to pull against. Instead, keep a steady contact with one rein and repeatedly 'give and take' on the other. This does not mean yanking and snatching on it, it means slightly reducing and increasing the degree of contact in a measured manner. If necessary, these actions on the reins can be alternated at intervals.

In rounding off this section, I want to refer back to the point I made earlier that even inexperienced riders have a responsibility to try to look after and control their horses to the best of their ability, and riding at speed in company is a prime example of this. If you are following other riders in single file, it is *your* responsibility not to let your horse charge into the back of the one in front, so you must look what you are doing and not get too close. (Apart from the danger of collision, there is a danger, on some tracks, of you or your horse being hit in the face by flying clods or loose stones.) Allowing your horse to barge past another in a narrow space is also a dangerous no-no. And if you are cantering line abreast across a field, keep a few yards of space between your horse and those alongside, to prevent any collision caused by deviation, or the possibility of one horse being kicked by another. Riding at speed should be fun for you, your horse and your fellow riders. Make a decision that the way you approach it helps ensure that this is so.

Up Hill and Down Dale

Because we are talking about 'early days' here, it is unlikely that readers will be taken across terrain that resembles the Grand Canyon, but is has to be acknowledged that not every area of the countryside is completely flat. Sooner or later, when riding out, you will be confronted with hills of some sort, and it is in both your interests and your horse's that you have an idea of how to ride them.

The most important points to remember about hills are:

1 The horse is 'rear-engined'.

2 The horse needs to retain his balance.

3 The horse will retain his own balance much more easily if the rider's position is stable, and the rider doesn't do anything that will interfere with the horse's movement.

Going uphill

Although going uphill requires more effort from the horse than moving on the flat it is, in mechanical terms, relatively uncomplicated for him, because his hindquarters, the source of his propulsive power, are well placed for pushing his own, and his rider's weight up the slope. (When riding a horse up a fairly steep hill, you will also notice extra activity in his shoulders. While this does help with overall movement, it happens chiefly because, since his forefeet are higher up the slope than his hind feet, he needs to raise his shoulders to take active steps in front.) Your role as the rider is to make the horse's task as easy as possible, and this entails:

1 Keeping the hindquarters and loins (the area between the back of the saddle and the hindquarters) unencumbered.

2 Keeping your own weight stable and as close as practical to the horse's centre of gravity (see Cantering in the Open).

Both these aims can be achieved by folding your upper body forward from the hips, and slightly lightening your seat will also help the horse's back to work freely. The amount you fold forward will depend upon the steepness of the slope, but the main criterion will be simply a feeling that you are in balance with the horse. If he is really working up the slope, he will want to stretch his head and neck forward and down, and your rein contact should be light and sensitive to this requirement.

In contrast to these correct criteria, it will be evident that a lazy rider who sits back in the saddle in a 'chair seat' (see Posture, not Posing) and hangs on to the reins will be making the horse's task far more difficult.

Going uphill, you should fold your upper body forward, lighten your seat and keep a light, sensitive rein contact to make the horse's task as easy as possible.

Going downhill

Going downhill in a measured, balanced fashion is not that easy for a horse, because he has to contend both with the effects of gravity and the fact that his hindquarters, the source of his propulsive power, are higher up the slope than the rest of him. If he doesn't take care to regulate his movement, he risks hurrying down the hill in a precipitate fashion.

However, a rider who responds to these points by simply hanging on to the horse's mouth is going to make the situation worse, not better. This is because, in order to retain his balance, it is very important that the horse is able to engage his hind legs underneath his body. If he can't do this, he risks more or less sliding down the hill, trying to 'prop himself up' with his forelegs, but with minimal control of his movement – pretty much at the mercy of gravity. As we saw earlier (Very Basic Mechanics of the Horse and Posture, not Posing), anything a rider does to make a horse go 'hollow' will interfere with his ability to engage his hind legs – and one of these things is pulling back on the reins. Therefore, what is needed from the rider is not a heavy contact on the reins but a light yet definite one that gives the horse a sort of 'point of reference' for his front end. Because the horse's head is lower than it would be on level ground, it also helps if the rider's hands are held quite low, to maintain a more or less straight line through elbows and hands to the bit.

Another thing that can help or hinder the horse's balance and movement is the rider's overall posture, which affects weight distribution on the horse. Getting this absolutely right can be quite difficult (one reason why novice riders shouldn't be expected to ride down steep slopes) but there are some useful guidelines:

- Leaning too far back can interfere with the freedom of the horse's loins, and thus with the activity of his hind limbs which, as we've seen, is unhelpful. Also, a rider who really leans back will tend to stick the lower legs forward in front of the girth, and this will make it hard to use them to keep the horse straight which, as we will see in a moment, can be very important.

- Folding forward (as when going uphill) may place the rider's weight in front of the horse's centre of gravity, which will make it difficult for the horse to keep moving in a balanced, measured way – and will also be precarious for the rider.

- The aim is to achieve a balanced position, the elements of which are shown in the illustration on page 156. The hill here is very steep, but this is an extreme example intended to emphasise the points to aim for.

Another point is that it is much easier for the horse going downhill to maintain his balance and regulate his movement if he keeps straight (his back end directly behind his front end). If his source of power comes out of alignment, it will push him askew (a bit like a rear-wheel skid) and he may lose control of his momentum and direction. Therefore, it is important that the rider helps to keep the horse straight and this is achieved by keeping straight yourself (not leaning to one side or the other) and by correcting any tendency for the horse to deviate off line by supporting him with your leg aids. As we saw earlier (Showing, not Steering) the hands have a minimal role in this because, if you try to straighten a horse by pulling on one rein, his back end is likely to swing in the opposite direction – which is *not* what you want to happen when going downhill.

In addition to keeping the horse straight, your legs should 'support' his forward movement – that is too say, they should be kept on his sides gently, literally to encourage him, but they shouldn't be used to 'drive' or 'nag' him. Especially when riding downhill on a slick or loose surface (for instance, on a wet metalled road or a pebble-strewn path) it is important not to 'bustle' the horse, because that's when he might hurry and slip.

Novice riders shouldn't be expected to go down hills anything like as steep as that shown but this picture, based on a partnership descending the Derby Bank at Hickstead, emphasises some important points. The rider is sitting in balance with the horse, not interfering by leaning too far forward or back (see vertical line through rider's shoulder, knee and horse's foreleg); he is looking ahead, not down; the rein contact is light, but just sufficient to steady the horse; rider's leg has maintained its position on the girth, from where it can act as necessary to help hold the horse straight. Note also how much the horse needs to engage his hind legs to retain balance down a steep hill.

Although well-trained, well-balanced, well-ridden horses can go down hill in all the gaits, because of the difficulties mentioned it is highly unlikely that novice riders will be expected to ride downhill in any gait other than walk.

So, That's the Beginning…

I suppose the final section in most books would be headed 'Conclusion' or similar, but I'd like to finish by making a different point. Once you can carry out the movements and exercises mentioned in this book with basic competence, and enjoy going on escorted hacks, you will have reached the starting point of what riding is really about. With continued practice and instruction you will, if you so wish, be able to make a start at jumping, dressage or the other mounted sports – and you will develop the skill to ride a greater variety of horses more proficiently. The last point is perhaps the key to what I'm saying here – throughout this book I hope you've noted repeated references to thinking, and communicating with the horse, as fundamental aspects of riding. Yes, the purely technical stuff *is* very important but, security aside, it is mainly about *enabling* effective communication. Riding has a lot in common with learning a language – what you have been doing up to this point is the equivalent of learning how to get by on a first foreign holiday: you can order the dinner you want without inadvertently insulting the waiter's sister and ask directions to the pool and not end up in the loo. Even if your grammar and sentence construction are a bit ropey, you can make yourself understood by someone who knows a few words of *your* language, and is trying to help you. In other words, you're not likely to do anything that will upset a laid-back riding school horse, and most of the time he can pretty much figure out what you want him to do.

This is fine as a starting point but, to continue the foreign holiday analogy, if you want to get really involved in the people and culture of another country, the more you learn about different aspects of that country, and the more you develop your powers of communication, the more readily you will be absorbed into the community. From the riding viewpoint, learning more about what 'makes horses tick', and refining your position and aiding, will set you along the road to communicating effectively with a greater variety of horses so you will, for instance, be able to ride more highly tuned, responsive horses and perhaps younger horses, who need more understanding, 'explanation' and direction from the saddle.

So, once you've achieved competence in the basics, rather than thinking: 'I can ride now', think: 'I'm starting to ride now.' I can assure you that you'll get far more fulfilment from the sport if you adopt this latter approach.

Useful Addresses

The organizations listed can provide details of riding centres approved by themselves in various parts of the UK, and may also be able to answer other queries relating to riding tuition.

Association of British Riding Schools (ABRS)
Address: Queen's Chambers, 38–40 Queen Street, Penzance, Cornwall TR18 4BH

Telephone: 01736 369 440
Website: www.abrs-info.org

British Horse Society (BHS)
Address: Stoneleigh Deer Park, Kenilworth, Warwickshire CV8 2XZ

Telephone: 01926 707700 (switchboard)
Website: www.bhs.org.uk

Riding for the Disabled Association (RDA)
Address: Lavinia Norfolk House, Avenue R, Stoneleigh Park, Stoneleigh, Kenilworth, Warwickshire CV8 2LY

Telephone: 0845 658 1082
Website: www.rda.org.uk

Index

above the bit 52, 54–5
accepting the contact 49
aids 4, 56–8, 62–4, 66, 147
arena (see also school) 5
Association of British Riding Schools
(ABRS) 12, 162

balance 36, 53, 58, 62, 71, 83, 90,
    92–6, 103, 110, 113, 153, 155
behind the bit 49
behind the movement 35, 43
bend 5, 110, 115–16, 119
    counterbend 9
British Horse Society (BHS) 12, 162

canter 79–84, 90, 91, 92, 143
    collected 85
    counter-canter 82
    disunited canter 81
centre of gravity 147–8, 151, 154, 155
centre of motion 42, 151
chair seat 34–6, 74, 95, 154
change the rein 5, 105-6
circles 82, 92, 105, 107, 110–17
clothing/kit 19–20
crotch seat 38–9

dead to the leg 46
diagonals 5
    diagonal in trot 76–7
    long diagonal across school 105–6
dismounting 21–3
dominant hand 51–2
driving seat 43, 72

falls 16–18
foetal position 36–7, 148
forehand, on the 7, 53, 71, 92–6, 117,
    120–3
fork seat (see also crotch seat) 148

gaits 6, 55, 70–92
girth 8, 21

hacking 77, 137–57
half-halt 96-8
halt 63, 86–8, 90, 123
hills 153

impulsion 6
incline 103–4
inside leg/rein (see also reins and leg
aids) 6, 66–9, 81–2, 114, 116, 120, 123

leading file 7, 24, 126
leading leg 9, 80, 86
leaning on the bit 52–3, 94–5
leg aids 44–6, 71–2, 76, 86, 88, 89, 97,
    119, 121, 129, 131, 142–3, 156
leg-yielding 115, 117–20
light seat 43
loaded seat (see also weighted seat)
    43
lunge 24, 78, 134–5

manège (see also arena and school) 5
marker letters 99–103
mounting 21–3
mouth 47–9, 66

neckstraps 26–7

outside leg/rein (see also reins and
leg aids) 7, 67–9, 81–2, 114, 116, 120,
    123
overbending 49–50

paces (see also gaits) 8
platform of balance 148–50
poised position 43, 147
position (posture) 33–41, 54, 73–4,
    135, 146–53 , 154–5

pulling 52, 53–4, 152
punishment 133–4

rear file 8, 126–7
reins (see also inside leg/rein and
    outside leg/rein) 8, 46–56, 64–5,
    67, 70, 86, 89, 95, 96, 97, 123, 124,
    130, 143, 155
rhythm 60–1, 71–2, 73–4, 110, 113
Riding for the Disabled (RDA) 15, 162
riding schools 1, 11–14, 17, 19, 24, 136
roads 73, 138–41

seat 26–7, 41–3 , 54, 69, 72, 78, 81–3,
    88, 89, 96–7, 151–2
school 13, 99
serpentines 105–8
shallow loop 103, 108–9
Spanish Riding School 50, 58
stirrup leathers 21, 74, 127–8, 139,
    149–51

tacking up 8, 135–6
transitions 8, 62–4, 71, 78, 80, 81, 83,
    84–92
trot 87, 90, 91
    extended 85
    sitting 77–9
    rising 73–7
turns 63–9, 82, 101, 114, 120–3

voice 143

walk 70-2, 87, 91
weighted seat (see also loaded seat)
    69
whip 20, 71, 129–35
    short 130–2
    dressage 131–2

Reader's Notes